After the Ascension
SPIRITUAL AND HUMANISTIC ESSAYS

By M. Grace Ferri

TATE PUBLISHING, LLC

After the Ascension by M. Grace Ferri

Copyright © 2005 by M. Grace Ferri. All rights reserved.

Published in the United States of America
by Tate Publishing, LLC
127 East Trade Center Terrace
Mustang, OK 73064
(888) 361–9473

Book design copyright © 2005 by Tate Publishing, LLC. All rights reserved. No part of this publication may be reproduced, stored in a retrieval system or transmitted in any way by any means, electronic, mechanical, photocopy, recording or otherwise without the prior permission of the author except as provided by USA copyright law.

Scripture quotations are taken from the *Holy Bible, New International Version* ®, Copyright © 1973, 1978, 1984 by International Bible Society. Used by permission of Zondervan Publishing House. All rights reserved.
The opinions expressed by the author are not necessarily those of Tate Publishing, LLC.

ISBN: 1–9332901–4-5

*This book is dedicated to my husband, John,
who stood by me through all my trials and tribulations.*

ACKNOWLEDGMENTS

I am grateful to the hundreds of writers and teachers who have shaped my life and helped me learn these truths. Most of all, I thank God for the privilege of sharing them with you.

I thank my typist, Pearl E. Ryan, who typed, retyped and retyped with patience and kindness. Unfortunately, Pearl became seriously ill and is now residing in a nursing home.

I am also grateful to Deborah J. Ashe who worked with me in "winding up" this book, not only with her typing, but with her email expertise and personal support.

I thank my family and all others who have supported me in this endeavor, including my granddaughter, Jenelle L. Ferri, a graduate of Syracuse University, Syracuse, New York for co-editing this book with me.

I also want to thank Paul T. Verduchi who was instrumental in finding and preparing the beautiful images in this book (Author's choices).

*I proclaim righteousness in
the great assembly;*

*I do not seal my lips,
as you know, oh Lord.*

*I do not hide your righteousness
in my heart;*

*I speak of your faithfulness
and salvation.*

*I do not conceal your love
and your truth from the great assembly.*

(Psalm 40:10–11)[1]

---

[1] BEING RIGHTEOUS DOES NOT MEAN ALWAYS BEING RIGHT. IT MEANS BEING RIGHT WITH GOD.

TABLE OF CONTENTS

It All Begins with the Bible 15
God Speaks in the Bible. 18
Picture of the Ascension. 20
God's Plan to Carry on His Son's Teachings. 21
Jesus Promises the Holy Spirit. 23
A Glorious Experience (Holy Spirit) 25
The Variety and The Unity of Spiritual Gifts. 27
Speaking in Tongues 29
An Emperor's Feat. 31
Brokenness. 34
Does God Heal Today? 37
Transform Your Heart 39
Jesus Teaches Nicodemus 42
Clarification of "Born Again" or "Saved" 43
Is Your Mouth Saved? 46
An Explanation of Repentance 48
Grace 50
What It Means to Have a Personal Relationship with Christ. .52
Regarding God's "Will". 54
The Devil Attacks Us. 57
Evil. 60
Good Judgment in God's Service 61
Prayer to God. 63
Union with God through Prayer. .64
Lord's Prayer 66
Hail Mary. 67

After the Ascension

A Prayer of Saint Francis of Assisi 68
Angels 70
Arts and Virtues 73
Anger 76
Friends 79
Knowledge and Order 81
Love (1-Corinthians 13:1, 13:4) 82
What Is Love? 83
Three Kinds of Love 84
Love and Marriage 86
The Ten Commandments 88
Clean Up Your Act (Sins) 90
Prisoners of Childhood 98
A Wake-Up Call 100
How Could We (Poem By M. Grace Ferri) 102
Turn Your Life Around (Poem By M. Grace Ferri) 103
Let Him In (Poem By M. Grace Ferri) 104
Highlights In The Life of Christ 105
God Sent Us a Savior 106
Mary Was Chosen 107
Baptism 110
The Sermon on the Mount (Beatitudes) 113
The Transfiguration 116
Picture of the Last Supper 119
The Last Supper 120
Agony in the Garden 122
Picture of The Cross of Christ 123
The Cross of Christ (Essay) 124

Who Killed Jesus? (A Personal Reflection) 127
The Resurrection 128
After the Resurrection 130
The Ascension 132
Apostle Paul. 133
Meeting with Jesus. 135
Right and Wrong (Poem). 138
Some Things Are Right (Roman Catholicism) 139
Some Things Are Wrong (Roman Catholicism) 142
Taste And Style (Roman Catholicism). 146
Priesthood (Catholic). 152
From Tradition to Truth (A Former Catholic Priest) 154
The Brain (Good Health Tips) 157
With God All Things Are Possible. .160
Birth of a Theory (Three Heavens) .161
Summary of Three Heavens (A Hypothesis) 163
Rebirth of a Theory (Reincarnation) 167
Favorite Quotes 172
The Human Race 176
America the Beautiful 177
Separation Between Church and State (A Complete Myth) .181
The Letter of Controversy 186
Anyway (Treat People Like Winners) 188
Peace of Mind 189
Become a Child of God 192
Introduction to the Book of Revelations 197
Pre-Rapture Conditions 199
The Grooming of the Anti-Christ. 201

After the Ascension

The Rapture 203
The Tribulation Period 205
Armageddon (An Interlude in the Tribulation Period) 207
The Millennium 209
Justice for All 211
Personal Summary 212
Glossary 215
Picture of Jesus 227
A Personal Analysis 229
Biblical Quote from 1-Peter 3:8–9 230
About the Author 231
Index 235

M. Grace Ferri

You will find that I reiterate Biblical principles
in this book in order to ingrain them more effectively.
After all, repetition is the "Mother" of Learning.

THE ENDNOTES CITED ARE VERY INFORMATIVE.

INTRODUCTION

There is no stronger message than the message of God's forgiveness and grace

I tried writing this book in a clear and comprehensible style. I know I am just a very "small" link in a big chain of Christianity. I feel so thankful to God for His great gift of salvation that I wish everyone in all the world might know and love Jesus. God's greatest wish is for everyone to be saved through His Son, Jesus Christ. This book was written so that Christians will better understand the "Word" according to God. It was never intended to suggest any change from one Christian church to another. However, its intention is to elevate the spiritual level within one's own Bible-teaching Christian Church and to become aware of what God expects of us in order to enter the Kingdom of Heaven. I hope with all my heart that this book will bring you to some kind of spiritual awakening. It is time to move forward into a new place, into the things of Jesus Christ.

Being "good" and "doing good works" is never enough to warrant salvation. However, once we are saved, these efforts are a result of a true love for God. Good works will count for rewards in Heaven and on earth **after** a faithful relationship with Jesus. Many know His story, but do not know Him personally. And for those who never knew Jesus personally, He may never have been revealed to them other than in a factual way. Also, the works of the Holy Spirit may have been hidden from them and through ignorance and denial of certain ministries many good people will not experience the joys of God's Kingdom. Unfortunately, too many are spiritually lost; they do not accept things of God and do not understand spiritual ways. There are three kinds of Christians—-lukewarm, good and better (Born Again). Respectfully, one of the efforts of this book is to elevate the lukewarm and good Christian to the best kind of Christian.

We are all walking in the amount of "light" that we

have. Unfortunately, too many people are comfortable with their current level of knowledge and are not growing spiritually and possibly, due to improper preachings and teachings, **remain spiritually stagnant.** I feel sad that many could be continuing with the incomplete message regarding salvation. If you have a relationship with Jesus, you already have been given everything you need for life and Godliness. Upon our death, there will be a private judgment by Jesus as to the destiny of our souls. **The final Judgment Day is yet to come and that will happen with the Second Coming of Jesus.**

Paul Speaking: "For we must all appear before the judgment seat of Christ, that each one may receive what is due him for the things done while in the body, whether good or bad." (2 Corinthians 5:10)

ARE YOU READY? ARE YOU PREPARED for the second coming of Christ when He will come for His "Elect"—His "Chosen" (the Born Again Christians)?[2] **Born Again Christians aren't perfect—they just try harder.**

M. Grace Ferri

WE WEREN'T PUT ON EARTH JUST TO PROCREATE, WE WERE PUT ON EARTH TO PREPARE FOR ETERNITY. THIS LIFE IS PREPARATION FOR THE NEXT, AND IN THE INTERIM, WE SHOULD ENJOY THE JOURNEY.

"Unless one is Born Again he cannot see the Kingdom of God." (John 3:3)

"For the Son of Man is going to come in His Father's glory with His angels and then He will reward each person according to what he has done."(Matthew 25:31–33)

---

[2]There are parts of this book that are **not** related strictly to the contents of the Bible. It includes essays that are of a personal nature. Hopefully, God will accept my good intentions. (MGF)

M. Grace Ferri

IT ALL BEGINS WITH THE BIBLE
(God Speaks in the Bible)

We are *not* complete Christians unless we believe that the Bible is the truth and nothing but the truth. It is the only way to live rightly before God. Since there is violence, murder, incest, betrayal and other evil acts that God disapproves of, it must be said that the evil in the Bible is too often taken **literally** by many as being "the way."[3] For example, in the Old Testament *"an eye for eye and tooth for tooth"* is **contrary** to what Jesus preached in the New Testament:

> *"But I tell you, do not resist an evil person. If someone strikes you on the right cheek, turn to him the other also. And if someone wants to sue you and take your tunic, let him have your cloak as well. If someone forces you to go one mile, go with him two miles." (Matthew 5:39–40)*

The "way" is that which is fashioned from God's revelations through His human instruments from both the law of Moses and other prophets of old. Everything that was written actually happened, but too many lived for the "flesh" and *not* for the "Spirit." However, the evil in the Bible is there also to teach us. Another example of Jesus speaking **contrary** to the Old Testament (regarding Moses) is:

> *"Why then," they (disciples) asked, "did Moses command that a man give his wife a certificate of divorce and send her away?" Jesus replied, "Moses permitted you to divorce your wives because your hearts were hard. But it was not*

> *this way from the beginning. I tell you that anyone who divorces his wife, except for marital unfaithfulness, and marries another woman commits adultery." (Matthew 19:7–9)*

In the **Old Testament** we find God struggling to reach the people through the prophets. These godly men paved the way for Christianity. All the gathered writings and records from the Old Testament came from songs, poems and prophets. The Ten Commandments given to Moses evidently did *not* make the strong impact that God wanted them to make. Hence, God sent His Son conceived by the Holy Spirit and born unto the Virgin Mary. Also, it was the Holy Spirit who was responsible for the inspiration and guidance in the writings of the Bible. You have heard, from the Old Testament, *"Love your neighbor and hate your enemy."* This is also **contrary** to what Jesus preached in the New Testament.

> *But I tell you: Love your enemies and pray for those who persecute you, that you may be sons of your Father in Heaven . . ." (Matthew 5:44, 45)*

The **New Testament** is based on God's direct communication to mankind through His Son Jesus. Its books have been written by humans through the divine inspiration of God. The teaching of Scripture never came by the will of man. Holy men of God spoke as they were moved by the Holy Spirit and fingers were guided by the Holy Ghost to write God's words to the human race. The full spiritual meaning of the "Old Testament" is *not* obvious except through the "New Testament." Both are incomplete without the other.

There are those who are gifted in the interpretation of the Bible, but most need proper teachers, such as evangelists and preachers to instruct and bring forth the messages of the Bible.

First we must be taught through disciplined instruction, and then we can establish a course of direction. Teaching is only completed when learning takes place and learning is effective only when practiced. Knowledge is useless unless it is used.

What we are is God's gift to us—what we become is our gift to God. Jesus came down to save the world, so He alone is our Lord and Savior. If Jesus and salvation are *not* a priority in our lives, we could be flirting with damnation. Strong messages of the Bible are to love God, love each other and to help the poor. **We should always "love" people, even though we may *not* "like" their ungodly ways.** This is how God treats us—HE ALWAYS LOVES THE SINNER, BUT ALWAYS HATES THE SIN. God can do anything, but He seldom tampers with our free will, which He gave us. We should use the Bible throughout our lives to discover many more ways that God speaks to us.

---

[3] The Law was given to men to show them their own evil hearts and that they need God and His way of salvation and power for living according to the Law.

After the Ascension

GOD SPEAKS IN THE BIBLE

(An Additional Rendition)

Certain ministries have *not* encouraged Bible study. A true church does and preaches that only through Jesus can we have salvation. (It is an unmerited gift from God).

Many comment that the Bible was written by ordinary men, so why should we believe them? The Bible was written through God and the Holy Spirit. He guided their fingers to write what was correct. God also used their individual personalities. Anyone who can "read," can read the Bible.[4] However, it is the illumination (spiritual understanding) that counts. It is meaningless to memorize the Scriptures unless the full spiritual meaning is captured.

The New Testament is the whole basis of God's new Law. It is the story of Jesus (and His story only). If we do *not* desire to know the reason for the suffering of the cross or the details of the "Resurrection" (faith at its fullest) and finally the "Ascension" and "After the Ascension," we should be encouraged to do so.

Almost everybody on earth can read the Bible in his own language. Just as God used His powerful Holy Spirit to create the heavens and earth and all living things, He also used it to direct the writings of the Bible. These writings are the "truth" (as recorded) but they are NOT always the "way." The "way" is the words spoken by God through the prophets of old in the Old Testament and through Jesus in the New Testament. If we follow God's spiritual laws, we automatically cover the laws of the land.

CHRISTIANITY IS NOT A RELIGION, IT IS A RELATIONSHIP WITH JESUS.

"Make me know thy ways O' Lord; teach me thy paths." (Psalm 25:4)

"Do unto others as you would have them do to you." (Luke 6:31)[5]

---

[4] Many homes possess a Bible, but too often it remains unopened and in many cases just collects dust.

[5] The Bible's Golden Rule is first. Second is what I call the "silver rule": "Do unto others as they might want done unto them." Both rules should reflect in **holy** ways only.

After the Ascension

THE ASCENSION

JESUS WHOSE BIRTH WAS A MIRACLE LEFT THE EARTH IN A MIRACULOUS FASHION.

M. Grace Ferri

GOD'S PLAN TO CARRY ON HIS SON'S TEACHINGS

AFTER THE ASCENSION the New Testament was compiled many years later. These gospel accounts were written by contemporaries of Jesus who had first-hand knowledge of His life and the events of the early church. *"We proclaim to you what we have seen and heard,"* said the apostles. New archeological discoveries in the field of Biblical studies have added weight to the evidence that the Gospels were written by contemporaries of Jesus. The Holy Spirit was instrumental in assisting them in the writings of the Gospel.

The Resurrection establishes Christ's authority and, thus, validates His teachings about the Bible and Himself. Paul minces no words about this: *"If Christ has not been raised, your faith is futile."* The Ascension witnessed by many gave Him great power and victory. The absence of this witnessed "rising" could have instilled doubts in some believers.

According to the Bible, the first contact Jesus had with His apostles (from the Kingdom of Heaven) was on **Pentecost Sunday**[6] when, through the Holy Spirit, His gifts were showered upon them. After Jesus left the earth, there would have to be a way for His works to be carried on throughout the world. Jesus had taught the Apostles well within the three years He spent with them on earth, and only some of His other followers were truly informed regarding His teachings. The beauty of God needed to be displayed.

So how did His word spread and keep abreast for over

After the Ascension

2,000 years? Firstly, Jesus would send His spirit to the apostles to quicken them into His service. They would represent Him when He was gone. The apostles could *not* give the Church divine life any more than chemicals could successfully make human life. Hence, the glorified Savior from Heaven sent upon the apostles His Holy Spirit, which took place on Pentecost Sunday. God wanted His Son's teachings to start immediately. Thanks to the Holy Spirit, Christ the Redeemer would be brought into the hearts of all who believed in Him. The nine gifts of the Holy Spirit are still alive today (Refer to essay entitled "The Variety and the Unity of Spiritual Gifts"), **but love is always first, for without love we are nothing.**[7]

Ever since Pentecost Sunday, Jesus has enabled believers to serve the Lord effectively, to live Godly lives, and to feel a deep sense of oneness with all who believe in Jesus Christ. We should be very thankful for Pentecost Sunday.

> *WHAT CHRIST DID FOR US*
> *THE HOLY SPIRIT DOES IN US.*

> *"And above all these put on Love, which binds everything together in perfect harmony. And let the peace of Christ rule in your hearts." (Colossians 3:14–15)*

> *"Now, if anyone does **not** have the Spirit of Christ, he is **not** His." (Romans 8:9)*

---

[6]Pentecost Sunday is seven weeks after Easter, and since Easter moves around on the calendar (due to a full moon situation), so does Pentecost Sunday.

[7]Many people go through life experiencing **only** a partial blessing from God because they stop short of complete obedience.

M. GRACE FERRI

JESUS PROMISES THE HOLY SPIRIT
(The Too Often Forgotten God)

Jesus told his apostles, **before His ascension**, that a Comforter would be sent to them to carry on His works and that He would *not* abandon them without further instruction.

> *"John baptized with water, but you will be baptized with the Holy Spirit." (Acts 11:16)*

> *"If you love me, you will obey what I command. And I will ask the Father, and He will give you another Counselor to be with you forever— the Spirit of Truth. I will not leave you as orphans."(John 14:15–17, 18)*

As already stated, Pentecost Sunday was the glorious day that the Holy Spirit, sent by our Lord Jesus Christ, descended upon the apostles and others. The gifts of the Holy Spirit were showered upon them and these gifts are still in full force today. The spiritual gifts are given only to "believers."

Once we give our lives to Christ, the Holy Spirit comes to us as our teacher, instructing us in the things of God. The Holy Spirit speaks through actions of Christians; He helps us speak boldly for Christ. When we learn to obey the Holy Spirit, He can use our deeds and actions for God's work in our world.

It was through the Holy Spirit that the New Testament was written and the good news was spread throughout many lands. Holy men of God wrote as they were moved by the Holy Ghost. The scriptures are *not* the thoughts of men, but the thoughts of God given to them through the Holy Spirit.

There are those who accept the complete Bible as the "truth" and others who just accept the Old Testament. And then there are those who reject both "old" and "new." Nevertheless, the word of the Lord lives on forever through the power and glory of the Holy Spirit.

We are *not* saved because of righteous things we do. But because of God's mercy (grace), we are saved through the rebirth and renewal by the Holy Spirit, poured out on us generously through Jesus Christ, our Savior. God works through His Son Jesus and Jesus works through the Holy Spirit.

There are many Christians who are *not* interested in growing in the Holy Spirit and who remain Baby Christians—never advancing, never pressing forward to learn, listen or practice the full truth of the Bible.

*LIVING TO CREATE AN EARTHLY LEGACY
IS A SHORT-SIGHTED GOAL.
A WISE USE OF TIME
IS TO BUILD AN ETERNAL LEGACY.*

"And so I tell you, every sin and blasphemy against the Spirit will not be forgiven. Anyone who speaks a word against the Son of Man will be forgiven, but anyone who speaks against the Holy Spirit will not be forgiven either in this age or the age to come." (Matthew 12:31–32)

M. Grace Ferri

A GLORIOUS EXPERIENCE

Why has God given the Holy Spirit to those who believe in Jesus? There are several correct answers: power to witness, power to live above sin, divine direction, and help for understanding the Scriptures. And there is another important one; serving God and our fellow humans. **IT IS TRUE THAT ALL CHRISTIANS HAVE THE HOLY SPIRIT**—He is actively involved in our regeneration (spiritual renewal or revival). **But *not* all Christians have Him in fullness**, an experience we call the baptism in the Holy Spirit. When the Spirit comes in fullness, we will most likely speak in a language we have *never* learned, just as the one hundred twenty people did on the first day of Pentecost.

> *"And they were all filled with the Holy Spirit and began to speak in foreign tongues, even as the Holy Spirit prompted them to speak." (Acts 2:4)*

But entering into the Spirit-filled life through the baptism in the Holy Spirit is just that—entering in. It is like walking through the front door of your house. You get through the door, but the entire house is there for you to live in; you do *not* have to camp at the doorway. In the Spirit-filled life are the gifts of the Spirit, the fruit of the Spirit and the lifestyle of power and significance through Christ. The Spirit-filled Christian ought to be a powerhouse for the Lord, a shining example of what God can do in and through a person. The extent to which that is true depends on us, on how much we yield ourselves to the Spirit.

> *"If we live by the Spirit, by the Spirit let us*

also walk. Let us not become desirous of vainglory, provoking one another, envying one another."(Galatians 5:25–26)

Many Christians receive the Holy Spirit's gift of speaking in tongues[8], but because of incomplete teachings in this area, they do *not* know what is happening to them. Some even consider it something from the devil and unfortunately through ignorance, dismiss this happening as unholy. What a shame!

WE CANNOT FULLY ENJOY THE GIFT
OF PHYSICAL LIFE
UNTIL WE HAVE RECEIVED THE GIFT
OF ETERNAL LIFE.

"Put on a new self, created in God's way in righteousness and holiness." (Ephesians 4:24)

---

[8]Speaking in tongues, **usually** the initial physical evidence of Baptism in the Holy Spirit, is biblically correct and doctrinally sound. However, there are those who have not received this spiritual gift and are still baptized in the Holy Spirit.

M. Grace Ferri

THE VARIETY AND THE UNITY OF SPIRITUAL GIFTS

There are a variety of gifts but always the same Spirit. There are all sorts of services to be done but always to the same Lord, working in all sorts of different ways in different people. It is the same God who is working in all of them. The particular way in which the Spirit is given to each person is for good purposes: One may have the **gift of wisdom** given to him by the same Spirit, another the **message of knowledge**, another may have the **gift of faith** given by the same Spirit, another, again, the **gift of healing** through this one Spirit, one of the **power of miracles**, another **prophecy**, another the **gift of recognizing Spirits**, another the **gift of tongues**, and another the **ability to interpret them.**

All these are the work of the same Spirit who distributes different gifts to different people just as God chooses. For those who are skeptical of these spiritual gifts, they are in the Bible (1 Corinthians 12:7–10). These gifts are *not* to be confused with "earthly gifts," like gifted doctors, musicians, teachers, artists, writers, etc. Many Christians believe that the spiritual gifts are really *not* for today. Many claiming they were just for Pentecost Sunday. This leads to much division amongst the "Church." How do we explain the physical evidence among many Christians even **today**?

Many Christians believe that the "gift of speaking in tongues" is the fulfillment of being baptized in the Holy Spirit, while other Christians believe it is a gift God gives us like all the other Spiritual Gifts.[9]

> WHAT ULTIMATELY MATTERS MOST WILL NOT BE WHAT OTHERS SAY ABOUT OUR LIFE, BUT WHAT GOD SAYS.

"All these are the work of one and the same Spirit, and He gives them to each one just as He determines." (1-Corinthians 12:11)

"But you will receive power when the Holy Spirit comes on you; and you will be my witness . . . to the ends of the earth." (Acts 1:8)

---

[9] Catholic Charismatic Groups (usually functioning out of church basements) do exercise the Spiritual Gifts. I have witnessed Catholic clergy attending these Groups, including their participation in Catholic Charismatic Rallies.

M. Grace Ferri

SPEAKING IN TONGUES

To many, the most confusing gift of the Spirit is the "speaking of tongues." This gift is associated with the first gift when someone is baptized in the Holy Spirit. There are two kinds of tongues. One sounds like a language from a foreign land that the person is completely unfamiliar with, and the other sound is an utterance of reverence. Speaking in tongues comes to you spontaneously through the Holy Spirit. Unless your tongues can be interpreted by someone (or possibly yourself), you are never to reveal your special gift to anyone. For if all were to speak together in their spiritual tongues, many people would consider you mad. It's a language of love between you and the Lord. It's edifying to the person. Naturally, those who receive this gift can't help feel a little special. In many cases, it's intimidating to those who feel they have led a religious and saintly life and they have *not* received this gift. It doesn't make them a lesser spiritual person, for as the Lord had said over and over again, ***"It doesn't matter how many spiritual gifts you receive, without 'love' you are nothing."* Love is always first.**

Also, Jesus reminds us that the spiritual gift of prophecy is much more important than the spiritual gift of tongues. However, the spiritual gift of prophecy is *not* the same gift that the prophets in the Old Testament exercised, as those prophets could foretell the future. Spiritual prophets talk to people for their improvement and their consolation. When called upon by the pastor, they speak with spiritual inspiration to edify the Church. These spiritual prophets are gifted with more than ordinary spiritual and moral insight. (Includes inspired spiritual poets). It is a known fact that many Christians were given the gift of tongues, but did *not* know what was happening to them as some Christian Churches keep this spiritual gift toned down.

Open up your hearts and let the Spirit in. Maybe you are a potential prophet or healer.[10] God is always out there recruiting. Don't let Satan discourage you. Jesus will *not* come to you unless you reach out to Him first. He is patiently waiting for you to open up your heart and let Him in and to be a true follower.

WE WERE MADE BY GOD AND FOR GOD—
AND UNTIL WE UNDERSTAND THIS LIFE WILL NEVER MAKE SENSE.

"All that the Father gives me will come to me, and whoever comes to me I will never drive away." (John 6:37)

Paul said: "I thank God that I speak in tongues more than all of you." (1 Corinthians 14:18) "I would like every one of you to speak in tongues, but I would rather have you prophesy." (1 Corinthians 14:5)

---

[10] I was made aware that **not** all Christians believe the Spiritual Gifts are for "today." Hence, how do we discern what is for "today" and what was for "that day"? Also, what about the Bible being the whole truth? The Bible **is** the truth as written, but is not always "the way." In my opinion, the New Testament is the final discernment by Jesus.

M. Grace Ferri

AN EMPEROR'S FEAT

(New Testament)

The following italicized passage is taken from *The Da Vinci Code* by Dan Brown.

*"Who **chose** which gospels to include? The fundamental irony of Christianity is that the Bible, as we know it today, was collated by the pagan Roman emperor, Constantine the Great. Constantine was not a Christian. He was a lifelong pagan who was baptized on his deathbed, too weak to protest.*[11]

In Constantine's day, Rome's official religion was sun worship—the cult of Sol Invictus, or the invincible sun, and Constantine was its head priest. Unfortunately for him, a growing religious turmoil was gripping Rome. Three centuries after the crucifixion of Jesus Christ, Christ's followers had multiplied exponentially. Christians and pagans began warring, and the conflict grew to such proportions that it threatened to rend Rome in two. Constantine decided something had to be done. In 325 A.D., he decided to unify Rome under a single religion, Christianity.

Why would a pagan emperor choose Christianity as the official religion? He did this because he was a very good businessman. He could see that Christianity was on the rise and he simply 'backed the winning horse.' Historians still marvel at the brilliance with which Constantine converted the sun-worshipping pagans to Christianity. By fusing pagan symbols, dates and rituals into the growing Christian tradition, he created a kind of hybrid religion that was acceptable to both parties.

The vestiges of pagan religion in Christian symbology are undeniable. Egyptian sun disks became the halos of Catholic saints. Even Christianity's weekly holy day was stolen from the pagans. Originally, Christianity honored the Jewish Sabbath of Saturday, but Constantine shifted it to coincide with the pagans' veneration day of the sun. To this day, most churchgoers attend services on

After the Ascension

Sunday morning with no idea that they are there because of the pagan sun god's weekly tribute, Sun day.

Because Constantine upgraded Jesus' status almost four centuries after Jesus' death, thousands of documents already existed chronicling His life as a mortal man. To rewrite the history books, Constantine knew he would need a bold stroke. From this sprang the most profound moment in Christian history. Constantine commissioned and financed a new Bible, which omitted those gospels that spoke of Christ's human traits and embellished those gospels that made Him godlike. The earlier gospels were outlawed, gathered up and burned. Anyone who chose the forbidden gospels over Constantine's version was deemed a heretic. The Latin word haereticus means "choice." Those who chose the original history of Christ were the world's first heretics.

*Fortunately for historians, some of the gospels that Constantine attempted to eradicate managed to survive. The Dead Sea Scrolls were found in the 1950's hidden in a cave near Qumran in the Judean desert and the Coptic Scrolls in 1945 at Nag Hammadi. These documents speak of Christ's ministry in very human terms. It is important to remember that the modern church's desire to suppress these documents comes from a **sincere belief** in their established view of Christ. The Vatican is made up of deeply pious men who truly believe these contrary documents could only be **false** testimony, which is understandable as Constantine's Bible had been their truth for ages.*

*The vast majority of educated Christians know the history of their faith. Jesus was indeed a great and powerful man. Constantine underhanded political maneuvers do not diminish the majesty of Christ's life. **Nobody is saying Christ was a fraud or denying that He walked the earth and inspired millions to better lives and that He was the Son of God.** All it means is that Constantine took advantage of Christ's substantial influence and importance, and in doing so, **he shaped the face of Christianity** as we know it today."*

M. GRACE FERRI

LIVING FOR GOD'S GLORY IS THE GREATEST ACHIEVEMENT WE CAN ACCOMPLISH IN OUR LIVES.

"And whatever you do, whether in word or deed, do it all in the name of the Lord Jesus, giving thanks to God the Father through him." (Colossians 3:17)

---

[11] Excerpts taken from the novel *The Da Vinci Code* by Dan Brown. Copyright 2003, Doubleday, New York, NY.

After the Ascension

BROKENNESS

(A Tool in the Hands of God)

THE MOST DIFFICULT THING FOR A TRUE BELIEVER TO DO IS TO GIVE THANKS AND PRAISE TO THE LORD (REMAINING POSITIVE) WHEN ADVERSITY STRIKES. We must trust in the Lord that bad things happen for a reason and that "Good" will come out of every "Bad" situation.

Adversity is a condition of suffering, destitution, or misfortune and could be caused either by carelessness, wrong choices or by divine intervention. Why does God make us a subject of brokenness? Because adversity is a great teacher. God uses our brokenness to reveal our need for Him and He is patient throughout the experience.

The enemy's "lie" is that God has removed His love, but God will never stop loving us. He also knows how long it will take to grasp the wondrous freedom that is ours through faith in His Son, the Lord Jesus Christ. God knows the end result of brokenness in your life and is committed to us to experience all the blessings He has for us. Any discipline we experience in times of brokenness is God's way of changing and preparing us for future services.

When adversity strikes, there are those who turn away from God. Others put themselves in neutral and just coast along getting "tuckered out" being obedient to God. **Despite adversity, there are those who become stronger in their faith, which is God's primary intention.**

You will soon discover that only Jesus Christ can take your weakness and turn it into strength, hope and honor. We all need the fellowship and love of family and friends, but only Jesus Christ can meet all our needs perfectly and completely. It may seem that the brokenness will continue forever, but it won't. It stops at the point when our spirit yields to God's will and He erases the heartfelt painfulness when He senses a true desire within us to obey His "will."

Satan's effort is for us to become discouraged and for us to give up. Satan is crushed when we accept Jesus as our Lord and Savior and strive to follow the "will" of God even though He has given us a broken heart. It has been said that only if you "hit the bottom of the barrel" will your eyes be opened to the glory of the Lord. Of course, God's ultimate goal for brokenness is spiritual victory.

NEVER GIVE UP:

" . . . For He (God) Himself has said, 'I will not in any way fail you nor give you up nor leave you without support. I will not, I will not, I will not in any degree leave you helpless, nor forsake nor let you down, relax My hold on you.—Assuredly not!'" (Hebrews 13:5b) (The Amplified Bible)

Most of the time, if there are no struggles, there will be no victory. However, it doesn't always have to take a tragedy to open our eyes to the power and majesty of God, but it does take a certain amount of willingness that causes one to ultimately surrender. Many times it is a quiet despair of the soul that causes one to seek Jesus. Of course, people who are stable and in control of their lives—those who have managed to acquire a fair amount of happiness, success, and wealth—see no need to surrender and in fact would deem the very idea absurd. Those in this category most likely do *not* realize that by not surrendering to God's plan of salvation, they are dismissing all chances for eternal life in heaven.

Of course, our first priority is to accept Jesus as our Lord and Savior. He is our Healer, our best Friend, and our Deliverer. Jesus changes lives—He doesn't leave them the same. Jesus is the Great Physician who specializes in tough cases. He offers restoration to those who deal with the pain of abuse. He offers strength and hope for the weary and overwhelmed. He is the one sure solution for all those who are confused, afraid, downcast or upset. It has been proven that Jesus is still in the miracle business.

BETTER THE STORM WITH CHRIST
THAN SMOOTH WATERS WITHOUT HIM.

"The righteous cry out and the Lord hears them . . . The Lord is close to the broken hearted and saves those who are crushed in spirit." (Psalm 34:17, 18)

"And the God of all grace, who called you to his eternal glory in Christ, after you have suffered a little while will himself restore you and make you strong, firm and steadfast. To him be the power for ever and ever. Amen." (1-Peter 5:10)

M. Grace Ferri

DOES GOD HEAL TODAY?

There are three types of healing:

A. Personal efforts stemming from the knowledge of natural remedies.
B. From doctors who prescribe proper medicines or perform successful operations and procedures. (Medicine is also a gift from God).
C. Supernatural (Divine) healings come from our Lord who is the greatest physician of all.

Some well-meaning Christians don't believe in spiritual healings, but many of us know differently. First, healing from God does not exclude the value and use of medicine.

The Bible indicates that God is willing to heal persons who seek Him for healing, but that God is *not* obliged to heal everyone. Why God will heal some persons and *not* others is often a mystery, but we should be confident that His will is accomplished either way. We should seek God for our healing, but if that healing is delayed, we should seek God for the lesson He would teach us through the circumstances of our sickness. Sometimes we diligently pray and fast for a healing only to realize that the Lord has another plan. It is to be realized that praying for God's healing does not mean that God is obligated to heal us. We approach God with our petition and we believe God for the answer in accordance with His will for each of our lives.

We need to forgive others or receive forgiveness before we can pray for our healing. At times we have **un**confessed sin in our lives or we are holding grudges in unforgiveness towards others. These can obstruct our healing, but this isn't always the case. **Many times healing doesn't occur because the Lord has something else He wants to teach us or do with us.** If we want to petition the Lord with a free conscience, we should confess all known sin and repent. We should forgive any person we have knowingly offended and who still needs our apology. When conflicts are handled correctly, we grow closer to each other.

We have access to God the Father, through Jesus Christ, to pray for God's healing *not* only for ourselves, but for God's healings of others. Many people have been miraculously healed, *not* only by those in the ministry, but by the laying of hands by ordinary people who are in Christ. We all have family and friends that are "hurting." When we pray for a healing, we should mention that regardless of the outcome we will serve Him forever.

> CHARACTER IS BOTH DEVELOPED AND
> REVEALED BY TESTS,
> AND ALL OF LIFE IS A TEST.

Jesus Speaking To The Apostles

"The Kingdom of Heaven is near. Heal the sick, raise the dead, cleanse those who have leprosy, drive out demons. Freely you have received, freely give."(Matthew 10:7–8)

One Of The Nine Gifts Of The Spirit

". . . to another gifts of healing by that one spirit." (1 Corinthians 12:9)

TRANSFORM YOUR HEART

(Give Your Heart to Jesus)

"We can stand in a garage and not be a car,
We can stand in a stall and not be a horse,
We can sit in a ballpark and not be a team player,
We can sit in a church and not be saved." (MGF)

Death should remind us that we are pilgrims on this earth. Our real home is in God's Kingdom. The patience of Jesus should help us reach our spiritual goal, which is the promise of Heaven. **A heart that seeks Jesus finds Him,** and the goal of every person should be to have the desire to be with Him one day in Paradise (everlasting life). Sadly, too many, including lukewarm Christians, are unaware of just how this Holy mission can be accomplished.

Ask and it will be given to you;
Seek and you will find;
Knock and the door will be opened to you."
(Matthew 7:7)

Many are taught through religious teachings that to gain Everlasting Life after physical death is to "Be Good and Do Good Works" on earth. **Man's work "alone" counts for *nothing* unless firstly we accept Jesus as our Lord and Savior, placing Him above all others.**

"Anyone who loves his father or mother more than me is not worthy of me; anyone who loves his son or daughter more than me is not worthy of me." (Matthew 10:37)

One might think that going to church regularly, paying tithes, faithfully saying daily prayer, following both the Ten Commandments and the Golden Rule, being charitable, giving thanks to the Lord, along with even loving God the Father and striving *not* to sin, would clear the pathway to the Kingdom of Heaven. Without having a personal relationship with Jesus, *none* of the good works mentioned will position us to receive the grace of God. God gives His grace only to those who desire it. He is willing to "save" you as soon as you respond.

Just what do we have to do to be saved or born again in order to achieve everlasting life with Jesus in the Kingdom of Heaven? We must remember that God does *not* go where He is *not* wanted. Therefore, until we **hunger**, until we **thirst**, and until we **search** for the TRUTHS regarding salvation, nothing will happen to cause us to receive God's grace, which is a free gift given to us out of God's Love and Mercy. It is given only to those who idolize and worship His Son, Jesus.

As stated many, many times, we can only be saved by the grace of God. God's grace goes to those who want to turn their life completely around. This can be done by accepting Jesus as our Lord and Savior and by being truly remorseful for all our sins, along with confessing to the Lord and repenting. (Refer to essay entitled *"Repentance."*) **We are forgiven by the Lord only when we forgive others.** Confessing, repenting and forgiving have to take place soon after a sin has been committed. This should take place up until our last breath in order to reach our "goal," which is to eventually be with Jesus in the Kingdom of Heaven.

Once we surrender our life to Jesus, the Holy Spirit comes to us as our teacher instructing us in things of God. (Refer to essay entitled *"Jesus Promises the Holy Spirit."*) Being saved is much more than just **calling** on the name of Jesus (as some clergy preach). It means getting to **know** Jesus personally and *not* just to know **about** Him or His story. (Refer to essay entitled *"What It Means to Have a Personal Relationship With Jesus."*) Again, God's greatest wish is for all to be saved, and we will *not* be saved until we move from darkness to light by following His Son, Jesus. Also, after you are converted, you do *not* just speak in tongues; you do *not* just carry a Bible around (quoting scripture) or wear a big cross around your neck. However, you are to **strive** to follow the complete word of the Lord and speak the word of God to *un*believers, including lukewarm Christians who tether back and forth between God and Satan. Many may be turned off by your Christian efforts, but do *not* let the rejection shatter you. You will probably lose many friends, but do *not* get discouraged. **And because of our deep devotion and intense love for Jesus, our love will be stronger and richer for others.** We can make a spiritual change up until the last seconds of our lives as did the thief on the cross next to Jesus.

THE HEART OF THE PROBLEM IS THE PROBLEM OF MAN'S HEART

"May the Lord direct your hearts into God's love and Christ's perseverance." (1 Chronicles 29:18)

"And do not be conformed to this world, be transformed by the renewing of your mind." (Romans 12:2)

After the Ascension

JESUS TEACHES NICODEMUS

The ultimate words from the Bible regarding Born Again

Now there was a man of the Pharisees named Nicodemus, a member of the Jewish ruling council. He came to Jesus at night and said, "Rabbi, we know you are a teacher who has come from God. For no one could perform the miraculous signs you are doing if God were not with him." In reply Jesus declared, **"I tell you the truth, no one can see the kingdom of God unless he is born again."**

"How can a man be born when he is old?" Nicodemus asked. "Surely he cannot enter a second time into his mother's womb to be born again?" Jesus answered, **"I tell you the truth, no one can enter the kingdom of God unless he is born of water and the Spirit. Flesh gives birth to flesh, but the Spirit gives birth to the spirit. You should not be surprised at my saying, 'You must be born again.' The wind blows wherever it pleases. You hear its sound, but you cannot tell where it comes from or where it is going. So it is with everyone born of the Spirit."** *(John 3:1–8)*

M. Grace Ferri

CLARIFICATION OF "BORN AGAIN" OR "SAVED"

(Purification)

Why do so many so-called Christians cringe at the phrase *"Born Again," "Reborn"* or *"Renewed in the Spirit"*? Stemming from many personal conversations, it became obvious that many Christians lack understanding as to what "Born Again" really means.

Born Again Christians do *not* belong to an unholy cult and are *not* members of an alienated church. It is a renewed interest in Jesus, Son of God. Born Again Christians are the ones that the Lord admires the most for they are His saints and their souls are destined for the Kingdom of Heaven. This is proven in the Bible where Jesus speaks to Nicodemus: *"I tell you the truth, no one can see the Kingdom of God unless he is born again."* (John 1:13) Also, *"Ye must be born again."* (John 3:7)

Becoming a Born Again Christian means loving Jesus above all others and being a Holy Spirit indwelt believer in Christ. There is no greater way to live this human life than to believe in Him, the Supreme "Good." By doing this, He can turn our lives around and help us to keep His godly ways. We must let go of our ungodly ways and make a sincere effort to rid ourselves of all sins by confessing to the Lord, repenting and **striving** never to sin again. But being human, we will falter. Hence, because of the event of the "Cross of Jesus," we can be forgiven over and over again by God for repeated sins. We have to ask Him for forgiveness, for He does *not* forgive us without our asking. **Forgiveness is the greatest power the planet will ever know.** Confessing without sincerity doesn't work in God's eyes, for He knows the truth of the matter. However, one ongoing sin that you may *not* want to get rid of can keep you from the Kingdom of Heaven. Although we have the chance to confess and repent up until our last breath, this option could be taken away from us with accidents resulting in instant death. After death, upon the first judgment by Jesus, we will no longer be able to instantly achieve salvation. Therefore, being prepared is a better holy choice. **A true Christian would *not* harbor one ongoing sin forever for he knows the consequences of *not* confessing and repenting.**

> *"Those whose steps are guided by the Lord; whose way God approves may stumble but they will never fail, for the Lord holds their hand."*
> *(Psalm 37:23–24)*

After accepting Jesus as your Lord and Savior and **after** you cleanse your soul by confessing and repenting, your thinking will slowly be transformed into Christ's way of thinking. Jesus' outlook on life will replace yours; so will your manner of talking and acting. Your old self should gradually vanish and a new self (reborn) will eventually take its place. All this will come about with the help of His grace. You will become a loyal friend of Jesus, **striving** to live in constant union with Him.

Only **after** you form a personal relationship with Jesus do "good works" come into play. Good works alone can *never* get you into the Kingdom of Heaven. God wants us to follow

His Holy Spirit's direction and do whatever good we can do, for we only pass through this lifetime but once.

When you become a new creature in Christ, the Lord does *not* expect you to be low-keyed and passive (unless this was your personality to begin with). Our personality, as a rule, remains the same. What changes are attitudes and ways of thinking in regard to Christ in following His Father's will.[12]

In conclusion, becoming a Born Again Christian does *not* involve belonging to any special denomination, cult or group. It is a personal blessed achievement that God hopes "all" will become by falling in love with His Son Jesus Christ. He also wants us to become Christ-like so that we will be prepared to enter the hereafter to be with His Son forever.

> THE WAY YOU THINK DETERMINES
> THE WAY YOU FEEL,
> AND THE WAY YOU FEEL INFLUENCES
> THE WAY YOU ACT.

"For God did not send his Son into the world to condemn the world, but to save the world through Him." (John 3:17)

"For even the Son of Man did not come to be served, but to serve, and to give his life as a ransom for many." (Mark 10:45)

---

[12] There are many people who are claiming to be Christians but are portraying a different kind of Christ and who are not really "striving" for Spiritual Perfection.

After the Ascension

IS YOUR MOUTH SAVED?

(A Daily Challenge)

The following italicized passage is taken from *Me and My Big Mouth* by Joyce Meyer.

"It is possible to be spiritually saved and not sound like it. An individual can be a child of God, and yet not talk like one. It is not enough to be saved, the mouth must be saved also. Satan is looking for any tiny crack he can crawl through in our lives, and he loves it when we include losing control of our mouths. As "babies in Christ" we usually do not know how to talk spiritually correctly. Just as natural babies must learn to speak the language of their elders, so Christians must learn how to talk God's way. God will heal our mouths, but first we must realize we need healing.[13]

Unfortunately, complaining is a major problem among most believers. The word of God has a great deal to say about thanksgiving, which is the antidote for the poison of complaining. Many of us have attempted to call on the power of Jesus to help us, while at the same time our lives are full of complaining which weakens our spirit, whereas, thanksgiving releases the power to bring answers to prayers. **Being thankful shows maturity by being obedient to the Lord and honoring His Word.**

There are those of us who want to be used by God, but who feel that we just have too many flaws. **God will always look for someone who has a perfect heart toward Him, not necessarily someone who has a perfect performance before Him.** *Then there are those who usually say and do the right thing, but who do not have a "heart" for Jesus. However, Jesus is the only one who can judge our hearts and (to a degree) we can judge performances.*

The mouth gives expression either to the flesh or to the spirit. It can be used to verbalize God's word or it can be a vehicle to express the enemy's work. No child of God wants to be used as a mouthpiece for the devil, but many are doing just that.

There is no power in speaking God's word if the heart is full of unforgiveness, yet this problem is rampant among God's children. Multitudes of people who have accepted Christ as their personal savior fall into the deception of trying to operate one of God's principles while completely ignoring another.

If we want the blessings of God to be upon our lives, we just can't say whatever we want to say. We have to use our mouths to bless God, to bless others, and to bless ourselves. The mouth can be used to bring blessings or destruction not only to our own lives, but also the lives of many others.

Obedience to the Lord is the central theme of the Bible. For many of us, our lives were (or are) a mess due to disobedience. The disobedience may have been the result of ignorance or rebellion, but the only way out of the mess is repentance and a return to submission and obedience to the word of God. Bring your mouth into agreement with God and begin to walk in victory!"

THERE IS A DIFFERENCE BETWEEN EXPLAINING AND COMPLAINING

"I am purposed that my mouth shall not transgress. I will speak forth the righteousness and praise of God all the long day." (Psalm 35:28)

"Lying lips are extremely disgusting and hateful to the Lord, but they who deal faithfully are His delight." (Proverbs 12:22)

---

[13] Excerpts taken from the book *Me and My Big Mouth* by Joyce Meyer. Copyright 1997, Life In the Word, Inc. (Joyce Meyer recently changed the name of her television program to Enjoying Everyday Life).

After the Ascension

AN EXPLANATION OF REPENTANCE

(Become a Christian Champion)

Repentance implies a turning away from sin and turning to God. It is a change of mind whereby becoming a new creature in Christ and letting the old immoral ways disappear. It is far more than a few prayers. REPENTANCE IS ESSENTIAL FOR SALVATION. **We should confess and repent right after we realize the sin, *not* sometime later or once a week.** Of course, the promise to the Lord never to sin again is very important. As repeatedly stated, because of our weaknesses, should we duplicate the sin, we have to confess and repent all over again. Our sins are forgiven over and over by the Lord due to the ultimate sacrifice of Jesus on the Cross. God knows our hearts and we cannot fool Him with any false promises.

Unless we repent wholeheartedly, we will *not* be forgiven by the Lord. Repentance is the action or process of striving to eliminate misdeeds or moral shortcomings. It also means to dedicate one's self to the amendment of one's life, feeling much sorrow and the promise not to repeat the sin again.

However, there are certain sins that are *not* only spiritually wrong, but also legalistically wrong. These sins must be paid in full by paying the debt to society. God forgives all sinners instantly when they are truly repentant, but for those who steal, murder, rape, molest and deal in drugs, the price **must be paid** by going to jail under the judicial law. As mentioned before, even this group of people can become Born Again Christians if they receive God's offer of salvation and are truly remorseful.

Because of what happened on the cross of Jesus, we now have the privilege of being able to confess and repent for the favor of God's forgiveness.

THE HUMAN SPIRIT OF PERFECTION CAN MESS US UP— LOOKING FOR PERFECTION IN OTHERS CAN BE DAMAGING TO OUR HOLY SPIRIT.

Peter Speaking "Repent and be baptized, every one of you, in the name of Jesus Christ for the forgiveness of your sins. And you will receive the gift of the Holy Spirit." (Acts 2:38)

"If we confess and repent our sins, He is faithful and just to forgive us our sins and to cleanse us from all unrighteousness." (1-John 1:9)

After the Ascension

GRACE

(God's Unmerited Gift)

Grace is an unmerited divine favor given to us for our spiritual renewal or revival, which means to change radically for the better. The grace of God, next to God Himself, is our precious possession. With His actual graces, God speaks to us, draws us on to our true eternal greatness and gives us the strength to do spiritual God-like deeds.

When we receive actual graces, our mind receives holy thoughts, our will has good desires and we strongly feel drawn to Jesus. Such graces are special gifts. They help us to rise above earthly attractions and worldly satisfactions.

Natural gifts and talents are possessed by both good and bad people. Sanctifying grace, however, is only possessed by those who are in the state of growing in "divine grace" as a result of a commitment to Christians living before God. So great is this gift of grace that neither the power of miracles, the gift of prophecy, nor any other gift or talent can compare with it. This grace changes us and makes us more like Jesus. Without it we remain bound to earth and are controlled by human nature.

We should learn the difference between the mistaken desires of nature and the truly good desires which God sends us through His grace. **Nature is afraid of shame, contempt or insults. Grace does *not* mind such things because it cannot forget how much shame, contempt, and insults Jesus embraced for the sins of men.** We should pray to the Lord to become what we should have been long before now and to lead us on in regard to Heaven's glorious life. When grace becomes the ruling force in our daily life, only then should we have the wonderful peace of Christ.

And how does God choose those whom He gives this gift of grace? It is ours for the asking. God does *not* go where He is *not* wanted. However, there are exceptions to the rule as in Divine Intervention.

THE GRACE THAT ENABLED US TO SAY YES TO CHRIST ENABLES US TO SAY NO TO SIN.

> *"For by grace are ye saved through faith and that not of yourselves; it is the gift of God, not of works, lest any man should boast." (Ephesians 2:8–9)*

> *"Behold, I (Jesus) stand at the door and knock. If any man hear my voice and open the door, I will come into him, and will sup with him, and him with me." (Revelations 3:20)*

After the Ascension

WHAT IT MEANS TO HAVE A PERSONAL RELATIONSHIP WITH CHRIST

Having a personal relationship with Christ is having a loyal, loving attachment to Jesus and to His Holy Spirit by faith. We not only have to admire Him, we have to follow Him daily. Without Jesus in our lives, we can do nothing worthy of God's Kingdom. What our Heavenly Father wants is for us to abide in His Son Jesus Christ and allow Him to live in us. Only then will we be rewarded Everlasting Life with Jesus in the Kingdom of Heaven.

Time is so short we should *not* waste any more of it with half-hearted efforts. **We should *not* allow adversity to let us get sluggish in our love for our Lord. Whatever we endure on earth is a very small price to pay for the Kingdom of Heaven.** Bring your joys and sorrows to Jesus. Make Him your best friend and your closest companion. There is no other redeemer of men than Jesus. He alone is necessary. He alone can forgive us of our sins.

The foundation of our relationship with Jesus is His forgiveness to us and consequently our forgiveness to others. Only **after** we have committed our life to Jesus will our earthly good works make a difference in the Kingdom of Heaven where we will be rewarded accordingly by the Lord.

A great many Christians are slaves to a deep rooted habit of doubting; *not* doubts as to the existence of God or the truths of the Bible, but doubts as to their own personal relations with Jesus (in whom they profess to believe). They also have doubts as to the forgiveness of their sins, doubts as to their hopes of heaven, and doubts about their own inward experience. Those who have these doubts should pray intensely to God for faith in Jesus Christ and when they have been justified through faith, they will have peace with God through our Lord Jesus Christ.

When we are *not* in love, we take on a demeanor of "indifference." On the other hand, when we are in love, we express our love. We talk civilly; we listen attentively. So it should be that way with the Lord. We should ask the Lord to teach us how to build a relationship. **We should read and listen to the word of God. We must confess and repent as we walk away from sin—whereby making our lives God-centered and *not* self-centered.**

MOST PEOPLE ARE DRIVEN BY MATERIALISM. FOCUSING ON OURSELVES WILL *NEVER* REVEAL OUR LIFE'S PURPOSE.

> *"Love the Lord your God with all your heart and with all your soul and with all your mind. This is the first and greatest commandment. And the second is like it: Love your neighbor as yourself. All the law and the prophets hang on these two commandments." (Matthew 22:37–40)*

> *"Always be full of joy in the Lord, I say, rejoice! Let everyone see that you are unselfish and considerate in all you do. Remember that the Lord is coming soon. Don't worry about anything, instead, pray about everything. Tell God your needs and don't forget to thank Him for his answers." (Philippians 4:4–6)*

After the Ascension

REGARDING GOD'S "WILL"

(For Us to Accept and Follow His Son)

There are those who do *not* know the true meaning of Christian living and could be in the dark as to the full scope of sinning. They think Christian living merely means going to church, saying a certain amount of prayers, and avoiding all so-called serious sins. One that does this much may think he has God dwelling in his soul, but such a person could be spiritually dead. Christian living begins with God's grace as a gift from God. One who seeks His grace strives to live more fully for God by being an imitator of Christ's earthly example. We should follow the "will" of the Heavenly Father as Jesus did. **We should try to think, speak, and act more like Jesus each day, and as loyal followers, we should try again and again in spite of repeated failures.** On the authority of God's word we can be assured that every sin will be forgiven when confessed in faith and with repentance. Living a spiritual life does *not* mean living it one day a week in church. We should live a spiritual life every day.

Jesus gave us a new commandment and that is *"to love one another as I love you."* The question is often asked, *"How can I love everybody when I dislike or even hate some hurtful wrongdoings?"* **The Lord's command is to love everyone. However, we do *not* have to like or accept their ungodly ways. We should always hate the sin, but never hate the sinner.** The Lord does *not* expect us to have a personal relationship with everyone. He does expect us to treat others as we would like to be treated, which is in a fair and civil manner along with being compassionate.

Start anew—keep your loving positive ways, but change your negative sinful ways. Many lukewarm Christians are familiar with the Ten Commandments and some church laws but are in the dark as to the full scope of sinning. **(Refer to essay entitled *"Clean Up Your Act."*)** It has to be repeated, at this point, that no matter how good we are and no matter how many virtues we have, *without* Christ in our lives, our good efforts will *not* earn us the privilege of one day being with Jesus in Paradise.

Many may ask, *"Why do I have to fall in love with Jesus in order to achieve the victory over sin which leads to Heaven? Why can't it be just the faith and adoration of God that matters?"* Because if you are claiming to be a Christian, you must include Christ in your life. The New Testament is the story of Christ and His story only. He is the Son of God who came down to earth to save us from damnation. Jesus was the one who suffered severely, was crucified, died, and was buried. He was the first person to rise and *never* die again and who ascended into Heaven in a bodily form. Jesus then sent the Holy Spirit to continue His works. If you do *not* believe this, then you are *not* a Christian.

THE GREATEST GIFT YOU CAN GIVE SOMEONE IS YOUR TIME

> *"The world and its desires pass away, but the man who does the will of God lives forever."*
> *(1 John 2:17)*

After the Ascension

"For my Father's will is that everyone who looks to the Son and believes in Him shall have eternal life, and I will raise him up at the last day." (John 6:40)

M. Grace Ferri

THE DEVIL ATTACKS US

The devil, also called Lucifer, Beelzebub, Satan and the Prince of Darkness, started out as an Angel of God, a creation of God, but this angel was jealous of God and the power God had and wanted to take His place. Lucifer tried to undermine God's character and credibility and wanted to take His place in Heaven. Hence, in His infinite wisdom, God denounced him as an angel, and along with some other angels who followed Lucifer, were fallen to the earth. Then Satan became known as god of the earth and the battle began between God of the Heavens (Holy Spirit) and god of the earth (Satan). The world is a mess due to sin and unfortunately it appears that Satan is having his "heyday" and is winning the battle.

Most of us are familiar with the story of Adam and Eve. God had intended for the earth to be paradise where never a tear would be shed. In other words, it could have been Heaven on Earth. However, the fallen angel, in the form of a snake, first convinced Eve and then Adam to sin by making them eat the fruit which God had forbidden them to eat. Because of this act of disobedience against God, He cursed planet Earth, and rather than being the paradise God planned, He changed His plan for planet Earth due to Adam and Eve's disobedience to Him. Hence, there would now be tears, sickness, misery, guilt, and death as opposed to the wonderful existence God had originally planned. Of course, because of the "free will" given to us by God, we can either follow the Heavenly Father or Satan.

Satan attacks us by confusing doctrine with false teachers and false doctrines. He persecutes Christians and makes it difficult for many to live a full Christian life. **Satan urges us to trust in ourselves and *not* God.** He also causes us to play hypocrite and attacks us to make us worldly. Satan wants us to act immorally and disobey God. The devil does *not* attack the **un**believers since he already has them under his power. The devil is the reason the world is so corrupt. He is the personal supreme spirit of evil, the tempter of mankind, the leader of all apostate angels and the ruler of Hell. The devil is also delighted when we are anxious, paranoid, fearful and wallow in self-pity.

Extremes are actually the devil's playground. If he cannot get a believer to totally ignore a truth and live in deception, his next tactic will be to get that believer so one-sided and out of balance with that truth that he or she will be no better off than before.

If we want the real victory, we should strive for BALANCE in every aspect of life. We should take time to work, rest, play, sleep and spend time with family. Most importantly, we should take time to pray. Also, we should balance our finances—getting some kind of help if we can't do it ourselves. Being out of balance with our finances can cause extreme problems in many areas.

Credit cards have become a national curse when used out of control. They can either be a balanced convenience or an unbalanced disaster. The devil is in his glory when he witnesses Christians losing control in any area, possibly causing EXTREME stress resulting in unhealthy situations both internally and externally. Maintaining balance in our lives can certainly lead us to happier and holier lives of which God approves. **In any case, the devil is determined to steal our joy.** Oftentimes, it is easy for us to blame the devil for something for which we are personally responsible.

How do Christians deal with it? We put on the full armor of God against the devil every day and strive to follow God's will through Jesus Christ, our Lord. Don't let the devil torment you with past mistakes. You will *not* go forward to victory if you dwell on the negative past. ONGOING disobedience to the Laws of the Lord will keep us away from God's presence. **We should also pray to the Lord for strength to rebuke Satan and to be rid of his demons.**

> DO NOT LET THE DEVIL STEAL YOUR JOY.
> ENJOY EACH DAY TO THE FULLEST
> AND HANDLE ADVERSITY WITH HOLINESS

"And these (evil) will go away into everlasting punishment, but the righteous into eternal life." (Matthew 25:46)

"Be well balanced, be vigilant and cautious at all times; for that enemy of yours, the devil, roams around like a lion roaring, seeking someone to seize upon and devour." (1 Peter 5:8)

After the Ascension

EVIL

(Slated For the Fires of Hell)

The way we are treated and taught from our infantile state makes a huge difference in what we become. If we are repeatedly treated unlovingly, unfairly, or severely abused in any way, we could very well become confused and unholy adults. Those who are in this category could unknowingly become the devil's advocates. But if somehow someone comes along to teach the truth of God's righteousness, they are indeed fortunate. For those who are self-seeking and who reject the truth and follow evil, there will be wrath and anger, there will be trouble and distress for every human being who does evil. They become filled with every kind of wickedness, greed and depravity. They are full of envy, murder, strife, deceit, shameful lusts and malice. The evil are God haters, insolent, arrogant and boastful. They invent ways of doing evil. They are senseless, faithless, heartless and ruthless. **Although they may know God's righteous degree, they *not* only continue to do these things, but also, of course, approve of others who practice them.** God's kindness leads us toward repentance, but because of a stubborn and unrepentant heart, they store up wrath against themselves for the day God's righteous judgment will be revealed.

THE BATTLE FOR SIN IS WON OR LOST IN YOUR MIND.

"God is angry with the wicked." (Psalm 7:11)

"Many will follow their shameful ways and will bring the way of truth into disrepute." (2 Peter 2:2)

M. GRACE FERRI

GOOD JUDGMENT IN GOD'S SERVICE

(Jesus is the Judge of All Mankind)

Too often it has been said, *"We should not judge"* or that perhaps, *"We are too judgmental."* This verbalized finger pointing can make a person feel very unholy. The truth of the matter is that we judge every day of our lives. It is *not* wrong to judge words and actions, good or bad. IT IS WHEN WE JUDGE THE HEART OF ANOTHER THAT WE ARE IN ERROR. ONLY GOD CAN JUDGE THIS.

As an eyewitness, judgment of wrongdoings may be beneficial in the eyes of the Lord. **Other times we should know all the facts before judgment is made.** Of course, for the most part, there are two sides to every story and only God knows the truth.

We should all practice good judgment in our daily lives. We should *not* strain and go to foolish extremes in our activities. When we have made God's direction our main goal, we shall begin to show balance and good judgment in our external actions and we should always follow the Lord's holy direction.

Assuming is akin to judging but has no sinful validity. It's just an annoyance at times. People who assume repetitively are making up the minds of others without knowing for sure the truth of the matter. Assuming often gives the person the outlet to do things in his or her own way. This is indirectly a manipulative situation. Honesty and straightforwardness are the best courses of action. It is *not* always easy to live up to the Lord's expectations. **We must never feel that we have reached the ultimate in our spiritual endeavors.**

The Lord, in all His wisdom and fair judgment, accepts the "hot" and the "cold." But He spits out the lukewarm Christians who tether back and forth between God and the devil, making up their own religious rules and gamble regarding their eternal existence. These people usually close their hearts to the truths of the Bible and scorn valid spiritual advice.

The "hot" are Born Again Christians (hot on fire for the Lord). The "cold" are poor, benighted heathens who never heard the Gospel. Others are unaware persons who never absorbed or understood the Gospel and remain ignorant through improper teachings or having *no* true spiritual guidance. **Punishment of the "cold" will be moderate, indeed, in contrast to the terrible fate of lukewarm Christians who knew the way of salvation, but deliberately refused it.**[14]

IF YOU WANT GOD TO GO WITH YOU,
YOU MUST GO WITH GOD.

"Whoever believes in the Son has eternal life, but whoever rejects the Son will not see life, for God's wrath remains on him." (John 3:36)

"For just as you judge and criticize and condemn others, you will be judged and criticized and condemned, and in accordance with the measure you dealt out to others, it will be dealt out again to you. (Matthew 7:1–2)

---

[14] I know the Lord doesn't particularly like it when we judge or criticize others. But when "wrong" is definitely being practiced, we should "try" to correct the situation. We should always depend on the Lord, through prayer, to guide us.

M. Grace Ferri

Dear God, we pray to You
For people in all the world,
For other nations,
For other races,
For people who think differently
And live differently.
Help us to respect, understand,
And love each other.
Let there be no hate among nations.
Forgive all injustice.
Let wars end.
Let Your message be proclaimed everywhere.
Give us peace.
Amen

After the Ascension

UNION WITH GOD THROUGH PRAYER

Prayers can bring solace, peace of mind and inner strength. In public prayer some recite the same words, express the same sentiments, and have the same tempo to form a group prayer. Singing spiritual songs and concentrating on the words is also a form of praying. **However, memorized prayers are useless unless the prayers are completely understood. The same applies to memorized scripture.**

In private prayers, no "two" pray quite the same. Each has his or her own personal touch in dealing with Jesus. Through ignorance, many people pray to the saints and only mention Jesus in formal prayers where His name appears. **They know ABOUT Jesus, but do *not* know Him personally.**

We can pray for sinners, blessings, healings, and the poor. We should praise Jesus and thank Him for all His goodness. Prayers bring heavenly light to our souls many times each day.

Prayer is a friendly chat with Jesus and brings respect for His infinite power and goodness. It also brings gratitude for His numerous gifts and desire for His mercy, His assistance and His friendship. Also, we should pray for the "lost" to come to Christ. Prayer is a powerful tool, but we also need to grow in serving God and place ourselves at his disposal. Of course, Jesus should always be the center of our lives, and we should continuously strive to follow His Father's will. **Let us pray in the power of the Spirit.**

Then there are those who pray for the dead. When we die, we are frozen (so to speak) in whatever spiritual state we were in up until our last breath. God may give us the opportunity to confess and repent for all our sins and sincerely come to Jesus just **before** we die. But we must consider fatal heart attacks, fatal vehicle crashes, drownings, and other freak accidents causing INSTANT death. **We all make our own spiritual destiny on earth and *no* amount of prayers (from loved ones), after our death, can elevate us to the Kingdom of Heaven to be with Jesus.**[15]

We should *not* delay putting our spiritual life in order, for we never know what the future has in store for us. We may *not* be as fortunate as the thief who was next to Jesus on the cross. He had a chance at the last minute to acknowledge his belief in Jesus, hence, was able to join Him and the Father in Heaven.

WE SHOULDN'T BE IMPATIENT WHEN PEOPLE DISAPPOINT US.
THERE MAY HAVE BEEN TIMES WHEN WE HAVE DISAPPOINTED OTHERS.

> *"Love your enemies, do good to those who hate you and pray for those who persecute you."* (Matthew 5:44)

> *"Do not rely on the prayers and help of others after your death."* (My Daily Bread, a Catholic booklet by Anthony J. Paone, S.J.)

After the Ascension

A Personal Morning Prayer

"Dear Lord, please let me put on my full suit of armor against the devil this day and every day, and let me **strive** always to follow thy Father's will."

"Lord's Prayer" from the Bible

(Matthew 6:9)

Jesus Talking to Disciples

*"Our Father in heaven,
hallowed be your name,
your kingdom come,
your will be done
on earth as it is in heaven.
Give us today our daily bread
Forgive us our debts,
as we also have forgiven
our debtors.
And lead us not into
temptation,
but deliver us from the evil one."*

Catholic Rendition
(Revised in Good Faith)

*"Our Father, who art in heaven,
hallowed be thy name:
thy kingdom come; thy will be done
on earth as it is in heaven.
Give us this day our daily bread:
and forgive us our trespasses
as we forgive those*

> *who trespass against us.*
> *And lead us not into temptation,*
> *but deliver us from evil. Amen."*

"For if you forgive men when they sin against you, your heavenly Father will also forgive you. But if you do not forgive men their sins, your Father will not forgive your sins." (Matthew 6:14–15)

"Hail Mary" from the Bible

(Luke 1:42)

Elizabeth, who was six months pregnant with John the Baptist, said to Mary, who had just become pregnant with Jesus through the Holy Spirit, in a loud voice, she exclaimed:

"Of all woman, you are the most blessed, and blessed is the fruit of your womb."

Catholic Rendition

> *"Hail Mary,[16] full of grace,*
> *the Lord is with thee—*
> *Blessed art thou among women*
> *and blessed is the fruit of thy womb, Jesus.*
> *Holy Mary, Mother of God, pray for us sinners,*
> *now and at the hour of our death. Amen."*

Mary's Song

(Luke 1:46–49)
And Mary said:

After the Ascension

"My soul glorifies the Lord
and my spirit rejoices in
God my Savior
for He has been mindful
of the humble state of his servant
From now on all generations
will call me blessed,
for the Mighty One has
done great things for me—
holy is his name . . ."

A Prayer Of Saint Francis Of Assisi
(Catholic Patron Saint)

*Lord, make me an instrument of Your peace
Where there is hatred, let me sow love;
Where there is injury, pardon;
Where there is doubt, faith;
Where there is despair, hope;
Where there is darkness, light;
And where there is sadness, joy.
O Divine Master,
Grant that I may not so much seek
To be consoled as to console;
To be understood as to understand;
To be loved as to love;
For it is in giving that we receive;
It is in pardoning that we are pardoned;
And it is in dying that we are born to eternal life.*

Saint Francis was born unto a wealthy father. Grew up to be a "playboy" of his time. Had many serious differences with his father. Gave up his wealth and took on a vow of poverty. Had many followers. Lived in caves and preached the gospel of Jesus to crowds of people. Jesus was his Idol and Savior. Prayed *to Jesus to suffer like He did and through supernatural divinity was pierced bodily in five different places as Jesus experienced on the Cross. Continued to preach in different churches and was greatly admired. Assembled the world's first Nativity scene—complete with live animals. Remained poor until his death. His good works and poetry lived on.[17]*

---

[15] Prayers for the dead are a "dead issue" and prayers for the living are a "live issue." However, a personal prayer exception for the souls of the departed could be: "Please, Dear Lord, have mercy on their souls."

[16] Jesus is our only intercessor to God. Also, the Catholic Rosary Beads should be (per decade) ten "Lord's Prayer" and one "Hail Mary." Our Blessed Mother would have wanted it this way. (MGF)

[17] The Lord does **not** expect us to imitate Saint Francis fully as we need the wealthy to help the poor. Jesus does, however, expect us to speak up in His name. Our lives can be rich regardless of what we possess.

After the Ascension

ANGELS

(The Mysterious Messengers)

The following italicized passage is taken from *Touched By Angels* by Eileen Elias Freeman.
"Angels are God's creations and it is from Him that they get their instructions. They are the mysterious messengers with divine intervention for earthly mortals.[18]

Angels, to many, are creatures out of mythology that are associated with Christian legends. Others have a certain image in mind that is based on our cultural and religious beliefs. For the average person, an angel is a being with wings and a beautiful halo, of great wisdom and who comes from a place called Heaven and occasionally appears on earth. Some believe that angels are humans who have been transformed or perfected in the afterlife and then return to earth. Then there are those who view angels as ideas of God or merely literary devices.

Because angels seem to exist in another dimension, much of what we believe about angels is speculation based on revered traditions held to be sacred or personal intuition/revelation. The sacred books of many of the world's greatest religious systems speak of angels. A simpler explanation could be that angels are another race of sentient, intelligent beings, different from humans, far more powerful, wiser and more involved. It is believed that angels are created by God to serve the Divine by helping to form and keep in existence our world and other heavenly bodies.

Not a single human being has ever become or will ever become an angel *no matter how pure or holy or evolved he or she might grow to be. What is so menial about being human that some feel we must be transformed into angels in order to achieve our greatest growth and development? The destiny of human beings exceeds that of angels by an indefinable great margin. If you have absorbed what has been written, you will fully understand the destiny of human beings. It often happens that people hear their* *angels speaking briefly to them or feel their touch without seeing anything. A true angel appearance should be more than an aura of light. It should have a hint of a figure within the light.*

There is nothing consistent about what an angel looks like. All we know is what they look like to the individual person. Everyone who has had an angelic encounter has seen something different. We may draw some interesting conclusions about what angels may look like if we look into the kinds of experiences people have had, including tantalizing hints and some interesting similarities. Any angel we see or hear or sense is only a translation of the original.

Given their inherent power, they can be anywhere they want in an instant. The idea of bird wings on an angel is not reality. The earliest representations or literary descriptions of angels do not show them with wings. So why does most art depict angels with wings? Artists, coming to paint angels for the first time, had virtually no models to go by. So artists turned toward the only models that they knew; those of the Greek and Latin classical sculptors and painters who were accustomed to portraying Mercury or Hermes, the messengers of the gods, with wings either on his sandals or his helmet. All winged figures like Nike and Eros went into the making of angels in art. Since many experience seeing angels with wings, all they see is an appearance, an approximation of what is really an angel.

*In fact, an angel may appear to us with or without wings in whatever way it feels is most calculated to draw our attention, to listen to its holy message and to **act** upon it. When angels take on a human appearance to help us or bring us holy messages, they never have wings. In fact, there is virtually nothing to distinguish them from any one of us. The 'vanishing angel,' after confrontation, is a common motive in people's encounters.*

Angels are not affected personally by the pain and evil that still exist on earth. They have a much greater vision than we do, and they know that in time, as we seek the ways of Love and Light, we will grow beyond such things.[19]

After the Ascension

However, one thing does affect them and that is when we mistakenly think of them as substitutes for the Light, as mini-gods, or as 'beings' to be worshipped or placated. For an angel, this is as close to pain as possible.

We must never put the important works and devotion of angels above our love, trust, devotion and faith in God. *We should never get so caught up in angel mania that we put them above the love and trust of God. Many have actually witnessed their personal guardian angels and even communicated with them. As reported by many, guardian angels usually appear as regular persons. The visit is usually a brief one. The testimony has been that it is not a frightful experience, but rather a glorious encounter."*

WHEN ANYTHING IN CREATION FULFILLS ITS PURPOSE, IT BRINGS GLORY TO GOD.

"In appearance (the angel) resembled a flash of lightening, while his garments were as dazzling as snow." (Matthew 28:3)

"At three o'clock I was home praying when a man in dazzling robes stood before me." (Acts 10:30)

"But after he (Joseph) had considered it (divorce) an angel of the Lord appeared to him in a dream."[20] *(Matthew 1:20)*

---

[18]Excerpts taken from the book *Touched By Angels* by Eileen Elias Freeman. Copyright 1993, Warner Books, Inc., New York, NY.

[19]One of God's great mysteries is the lack of presence of a guardian angel for the innocent children who are abused, raped and murdered. There is a reason for everything and maybe we will find out "why" when we join Jesus in life everlasting.

[20]Archangels (in the division of angels) are chief angels in the Celestial (Heavenly) Hierarchy, ranking above angels. Michael the Archangel is an example.

M. GRACE FERRI

ARTS AND VIRTUES

ART is a physical skill acquired by experience, study and observation. It is also the conscience use of skill and a creative imagination. Skill means the ability to use one's knowledge effectively and readily in a performance, as in a particular occupation, craft or trade.

The art of cooking is the number one art in existence, for we have to eat to live. Of course, this means cooking meals that are *not* only tasty, but nutritious and well-balanced. God wants us to be healthy, and it starts with what we eat and drink. For **"we are what we eat, drink and think."** Overeating is a sin called gluttony. Eating sensibly is important for many reasons, *not* only for our exterior being, but for our interior being as well. Of course, what we drink is in the same category as what we eat. Water is at the top of the list as to the best liquid for us. Healthy choices in moderation could serve us well. Of course, exercise along with good eating habits contribute to betterment on our behalf.

VIRTUE is possessing a particular moral excellence, goodness or worth and conforming to a standard of "right." It also is a commendable quality or trait. Faith, Hope and Charity are the virtues God wants us to have above all others.

Faith: When we firmly believe and trust in God. Also, we see God's wisdom guiding our lives at all times. What God sends is *not* always easy to understand. It may even seem unjust or foolish to those who are living only for this world. We must *not* depend on our natural judgment alone, but learn to consult

God in all matters of importance. Though we may be mocked and criticized for what God has commanded us to do, we must pray for the courage and strength to follow the "will" of God. We must hate what is wrong and fear all sin in our daily life. **HOWEVER, FAITH IS DEAD UNLESS ACTIVATED BY "WALKING IN LOVE."**

Hope: As long as we are on earth, we will have to make use of food, rest, medicine, recreation, companionship, etc. However, we should *not* make the mistake of considering these natural things as the only remedies of our various needs. Otherwise, we will place too much hope in them and expect more from them than they can give us. **Do *not* place too much hope in any person or thing on earth.** Use whatever you can honestly obtain to improve your earthly life, but do *not* live as though this life were the only life. We should place our main hope in Jesus and follow His Father's "will" as perfectly as we can. When earthly friends and remedies fail us, we are not to despair. We are to stand by Jesus and He will help us reach the all-satisfying success of God's Kingdom.

Charity: A person of charity is **patient** in many circumstances which arouse others to anger or disgust. A truly patient man is patient with everyone; he makes no exceptions. When compelled to defend his rights, he does so without harshness or meanness. His kindness brings encouragement to those who are afraid or downhearted. We do *not* lose our strength when we succumb to patience. Impatience is a servant of the enemy (Satan). The charitable person never envies those who have more earthly goods, greater talents or better success. In dealings with others, he is **considerate** and **fair**. True charity makes one **humble** enough to face all facts, even disagreeable ones. The humble man remains at peace when others find fault with him. He does *not* care what others think of him, but in all things he is eager to please God. He knows that God judges without error or misunderstanding and he seeks only His approval. If we strive to develop this glorious virtue of Charity in our daily lives, we may be rest assured that we are walking toward eternal life each moment of the day.[21]

A TRUE CHRISTIAN "BELIEVES," THOUGH HE MAY *NOT* ALWAYS "COMPREHEND," AND HOLDS BY FAITH WHAT HE CANNOT GRASP WITH HIS MIND.

> *"Faith is the substance of things hoped for, the evidence of the things not seen." (Hebrews 11:1)*

Without Love We Are Lost

> *"This is love for God: to obey his commands. And his commands are not burdensome, for everyone born of God overcomes the world. This is the victory that has overcome the world, even our faith." (1 John 5:2–4)*

---

[21] We all have weaknesses and God certainly is aware of this. But it is our love for God that makes us strive to be strong in faith and the "apple of his eye."

After the Ascension

ANGER

(Get Over It)

Watch any news telecast and one thing becomes obvious, we live in an angry world. And while *not* everyone struggles with outward bursts of anger, there is enough irrational behavior to send us back to the drawing board of life to see where we have gone wrong. Each of us can choose happiness over anger and frustration, but it requires a willingness on our part to be open and perhaps painfully honest about the disappointments and frustrations we face. And when people get angry, the results are **almost** always negative—even frightful.

Anger is a God-given capacity—an emotion which offers magnificent possibilities, but only when people use anger constructively will they be free to experience joy in their lives. If we are honest, we will admit that each of us has dealt with feelings of anger and frustration. Along the road of life there are many situations that can anger us—being accused unfairly, treated with contempt, ignored and abused verbally. Then there is "road rage"—being cut off in traffic, bumped, cursed at, and also being scared of the consequences regarding drunk drivers, drive-by shootings, those who speed, and even those using cell phones.[22]

Then there are those who even get angry with God for certain unfavorable happenings. Most of us have heard the words, *"Why did God allow this to happen to me?"* Even God's greatest saints were challenged with negative circumstances. We have to decide whether adversity will bring us "down" or if we will be "lifted" to a higher spiritual plane. Even God expresses His anger when man violates His law. Jesus became **angry** at the presence of the money changers who had set up shop in the temple. He also **cursed** the fig tree for failing to bear fruit. However, God does express anger in love and righteousness and He never holds grudges. He forgives and continues to love. Hence, we should all do as God does. When we explode in anger, **we should say we're sorry**, first to God and then to others. We should work through the issue with honest, open and fair communication. Anger in itself, like temptation, is *not* a sin, but when coupled with hostility, it could sabotage the mind whereby providing an opening for Satan with results that could be sinful.

In any conflict, we need to realize that the outcome is *not* in our hands. **No matter how hard we may try, we ultimately cannot force someone to listen or change.** We should practice the skill of being a good listener and try to imagine the perspective of the offender. Many times a person who hurts us is a victim of hurt himself. He may feel the only way to release that anger and "get back" at the world is to do the same thing to someone else. We should always forgive the offender even when we find it to be a difficult task.

Anger has many faces. Some are subtle and barely noticeable, while others are open for all to view. If anger is held inside and *not* released in the proper way (admission with a **holy** attitude), it becomes a gateway for various physical and emotional problems. Many harm their own self-esteem by telling themselves they are the reason others are mad or irritated. This is *not* always true. No one can make us feel anything. We alone choose anger; it is a matter of choice. We should pray to Jesus for guidance in all matters for He is the controlling factor in our lives.[23]

ANGER IS JUST ONE LETTER SHORT OF DANGER

> *"In your anger do not sin, do not let the sun go down while you are still angry and do not give the devil a foothold." (Ephesians 4:26–27)*

> *"Do not let any unwholesome talk come out of your mouths, but only what is helpful for building others up according to their needs, that it may benefit those who listen." (Ephesians 4:29)*

> *"Do not be quickly provoked in your spirit." (Matthew 5:22)*

---

[22] It's been advised to pull off to the side of the road when using your cell phone. Can you imagine the confusion in the breakdown lanes on the highways if this procedure were to be followed? A suggestion would be to promote "hands free" phones or while driving use your cell phone for emergencies only.

[23] There were times I didn't immediately realize the error of my ways. I either wrote a note of apology or made a phone call regarding the issue.

M. Grace Ferri

FRIENDS

There are true friends, there are fair-weather friends and then there are acquaintances. **However, if you are looking for the perfect friend, you will never find one.** Also, happiness consists *not* in the multitude of friends, but in their worth and value. A true friend loves unconditionally, even when in disagreement, and does *not* forsake in times of adversity.

From when we are very young, our friends can have a great influence on us. That is why it is best to know right from wrong. Starting at an early age, teenagers especially can go in the wrong direction. Being popular and "fitting in" could hinder their well-being if *not* handled correctly. We are all products of our upbringing, environment and peers. Therefore, friends should be chosen wisely.

If we are taught by parents, church or any other godly person as to what is right and what is wrong, we are indeed fortunate. **Our whole future could be "botched up" by taking ungodly advice from someone we admire.**

Today's world is fast and furious. Alcohol, drugs, violence, pornography, and perverted sex are all too prevalent. Young people especially are easily drawn into these situations. In many cases there is too much pressure put on them to succeed in different areas, whereby many young people are becoming extremely stressed out. Then there are those given too much too soon, trying to keep up with others in the way of material things. These conditions exist *not* only with teenagers, but also with adults. Our friends can either be a good or bad influence. It is up to us to show discretion in keeping a friend, as bad company promotes poor morals. *"A false friend and a shadow stay only while the sun shines."* Sometimes friends are people who have the same enemies. This is *not* a good situation. It brings to mind the quote, *"Birds of a feather flock together."*

In conclusion, friends **do** have an effect on our lives. A true friend is someone who heartfully shares all your troubles, all your gladness and all of your cares. They can become an obligation, can be a commitment, **but most of all, they can give us much joy.**

THE MORE YOU BECOME JESUS' FRIEND, THE MORE YOU WILL CARE ABOUT THE THINGS HE CARES ABOUT

"He who leads the upright along an evil path will fall into his own trap, but the blameless will receive a good inheritance." (Proverbs 28:10)

"Two are better off than one, because together they can work more effectively. If one of them falls down, the other can help him up . . . Two people can resist an attack that would defeat one person alone. A rope made of three cords is hard to break." (Ecclesiastes 4:9)

M. Grace Ferri

KNOWLEDGE AND ORDER

We should all strive to become more knowledgeable. Each of us is different as to the gifts God has given us. What we are is God's gift to us—what we become is our gift to God. Where there is aliveness of interest and purpose, growing old might mean growing wiser in mind and character and becoming more informed in matters relating to personal and common welfare. **However, any knowledge that isn't put to use is useless.** Maturity is *not* measured by intellect. It is measured by compassion, logic (common sense) and the love we have for God and each other. There should be no ending to our learning and growing. Most learned men are deeply aware that they know little. Unless learning leads ourselves and others to a better life (a life closer to God), it is a waste of precious time.

God loves order because order is born of intelligence. Where order is lacking, there can only be confusion and destruction. If we want to please God, we must put order into our lives. *Not* only must we obey the commands of God, but also orders that come through lawful superiors. **Only if the command is sinful must we refuse to be obedient.** Also, we need to be obedient *not* only to the Lord, but to our obligations in our daily lives. The chief job of our culture is to help all people grow up. The trick is to grow up before we grow old.

> *"Whoever loves discipline loves knowledge, but he who hates (legitimate) correction is stupid."*
> *(Proverbs 12:1)*

After the Ascension

"If we speak in tongues of men and of angels,
but have not love,
we are only a resounding gong
or a clanging symbol.
If we have the gift of prophecy
and can fathom all mysteries and all knowledge,
and if we have faith that can move mountains,
but have not love, we are nothing.
If we give all we possess to the poor
and surrender our body to the flame,
but have not love, we gain nothing."
(1 Corinthians 13:1)

"Love is patient, love is kind.
It does not envy. It does not boast.
It is not proud. It is not rude.
It is not self-seeking.
It is not easily angered.
It keeps no record of wrongs.
Love does not delight in evil,
but rejoices with the truth.
It always protects,
always trusts, always perseveres."
(1 Corinthians 13:4)

M. Grace Ferri

WHAT IS LOVE?

(God is Love)

Love is forgiveness, understanding, kindness, patience, sharing, fairness, honesty, hope and trust. Love is *not* being jealous of others good fortune, including celebrating in each other's happiness. Treating each other civilly (*not* bitterly) is also a loving gesture. Most importantly, love is having faith in God.

Loving those who are at times unlovable is in keeping with a spirit of Christ-like love. We should speak our minds, but in a kind, civil way. Civil means being adequate in courtesy and politeness. Of course, as Christians, we should always speak up for Jesus because of our love for Him.

The process of loving someone enough to ask questions and hear the other side does *not* mean excusing the behavior. You must still recognize the person's action as wrong and hurtful and then forgive. Only the Lord can work with a person's heart as you extend patience and love. Whatever the result, you can be sure of God's blessing as you seek His way of dealing with those who hurt you.

Jesus Speaking

"Love your enemies, do good to those who hate you and pray for those who persecute you."
(Matthew 5:44)

"Love they neighbor as you would love thyself."
(Matthew 22:39)

Unfortunately, there are many so-called believers who do *not* follow these commandments. Of course, if these commandments were followed, the world would be a much better place with understanding and forgiveness prevailing. But, sadly, too many are following what Satan prefers rather than what Jesus preached.

Three Kinds of Love

Conditional Love: Dependent upon conditions like "Don't cross me" or "Things will be okay as long as you act my way"—it is a "take a lot" and "give a little" situation. With this kind of love, understanding and forgiveness are usually scarce with unfairness prevailing. Ironically, even sinners claim to love those who love them.

Unconditional Love: Not limited. Always forgiving, totally faith-　ful. It is the way God loves us and the way　w e should love others.

Romantic Love: Beware of the addictive nature of romantic love. The kind of love that truly heals us emotionally and physically is *not* romantic love, but rather the unconditional love that comes from God. The love that heals is *not* sexual in nature, but spiritual.

The Lord tells us also to love our enemies. **However, we can Love an enemy without spending time with them or doing things for them.** God ALWAYS hates the sin, but NEVER hates the sinner, and we should do the same. MANY GET CONFUSED BY THE WORDS LOVE AND LIKE. WE SHOULD SHOW LOVE FOR ALL, **BUT LIKING IS A CHOICE.** For example, we do *not* have to like molesters, murderers, rapists, incompetent rulers or acts of selfishness and unfairness, etc.; but we should always love and pray for those who go against God's will.

However, human love does *not* erase human weakness, nor do faults mean that love has ceased. We should strive to be aware of our own faults and work at correcting the error of our ways, both spiritually and humanistically. But most of all, we should generously forgive others as Christ forgives us.[24]

> TO STAY IN THE CHANNEL OF BLESSING
> FOLLOW THE COURSE OF OBEDIENCE.
>
> *"... God is love, and he who dwells and continues in love dwells and continues in God, and God dwells and continues in him." (1-John 21:16)*
>
> *"Hatred stirs up strife, but love (for everyone) covers all sins." (Proverbs 10:12)*

---

[24] Love and compassion are more important than any other gifts the Lord may have given us. If we have Faith in all its fullness, **without** love we are "nothing" even if we have God's gifts galore.

After the Ascension

LOVE AND MARRIAGE

We should realize that marriage is a solemn lifetime commitment. We can be more successful if we enter into marriage carefully, firmly making up our minds that the relationship is for keeps.

Set Good Priorities—our relationship with God should always come **first**. To succeed in marriage, both people must be led to their own devotional life by the Lord.

Family should be a **second** priority. Within the family, our priority should be to our spouse first, and then to our children. When there is a loving, nurturing, stable relationship between husband and wife, the children feel safe and secure.

Our "job" should be our **third** priority. We should never place our work above our relationship with God or our commitment to our family. This can be difficult to practice, especially for those who feel strongly committed to their professions.

Marriage is *not* a relationship of one dominating another, but rather each individual having specific roles that compliment the other. It's *not* a question of selfish domination. Couples should work, live and walk side by side as partners, loving and admiring one another.

Remember, love is the only force that will override hatred, anger, bitterness and unforgiveness. It is *not* a feeling—it is a decision. We must freely give God's love especially in the form of FORGIVENESS.

M. Grace Ferri

OUR HATRED CAN TURN INTO LOVE
WHEN WE DO RIGHT TO THOSE WHO DO US WRONG.

"Dear Children, let us not love only with words or tongues, but only with actions and in truth." (1 John 3:18)

*"Wives be subject to your husbands as is right and fitting and your proper duty **in the Lord.**" (Colossians 3:18)*

"Husbands love your wives and do not be harsh or bitter or resentful toward them." (Colossians 3:19)

*"It's not how much we do, it's how much love **is in our actions.**" (Mother Teresa)*

After the Ascension

THE TEN COMMANDMENTS

(Deuteronomy 45:7–21)

1. Thou shalt have no other Gods before me.
2. Thou shalt not make unto thee any graven image.
3. Thou shalt not take the name of the Lord in vain.
4. Remember the Sabbath day, to keep it Holy.
5. Honor thy father and thy mother.
6. Thou shalt not kill.
7. Thou shalt not commit adultery.
8. Thou shalt not steal.
9. Thou shalt not bear false witness against thy neighbor.
10. Thou shalt not covet thy neighbor's house, nor thy neighbor's wife, nor his manservant, nor his maid servant, nor his ox, nor his ass, nor anything that is thy neighbor's.

These Commandments were chiseled into two stone tablets by God and given to Moses on the mountaintop. Evidently, at that time, they did *not* make the kind of impact that God thought they should since **true believers** of the Commandments were unfortunately limited to God's unfavorable degree. The Law was given to show mankind its depravity and need for God's help to live according to the Law.

When beloved Jesus walked the earth, He added these Commandments:

> *"Love the Lord, your God, with all your heart and with all your soul and with all your mind. This the first and greatest commandment, and the second is like it: Love your neighbor as yourself. All the laws and the prophets hang on these two commandments." (Matthew 22:37–40)*

Again, **love** was the whole theme of Jesus' existence on earth—to forgive even your enemies, to be charitable, which also means to share your wealth with the poor. Jesus was so concerned about the poor. He didn't want everybody poor because He knew he needed the wealthy to help the poor.[25] He just didn't want the wealthy to be greedy and hoard their money. Sharing is caring.

Money in itself is neither good nor bad. It is "good" if it is in the hands of good people. It is "bad" if it is in the hands of self-centered people. Providing for family only and forgetting the needy is unholy, **and when we trust in money instead of God, we are doomed.** Whether we have a little or whether we have a lot, obedience to God's plan is the way.

> THE SINNER HAS ONLY TWO OPTIONS;
> TO BE PARDONED OR PUNISHED.

> *"It is with difficulty that a rich man will enter the Kingdom of Heaven. It's easier for a camel to pass through the eye of a needle,[26] than for a rich man to enter the Kingdom of Heaven." (Matthew 10:24)*

> *"The way of a fool seems right to him, but a wise man listens to advice." (Proverbs 12:15)*

---

[25] Many financially prosperous people share their wealth in **minimal** ways and feel they are "okay" with the Lord.

[26] The "needle" is not the needle we know for sewing. It is an opening in a protective wall where people and smaller animals have access to, but a camel definitely cannot fit through.

After the Ascension

CLEAN UP YOUR ACT

(A Clarification of Sins)

The Greatest Sin is the Rejection of Jesus, Son of God

All sins are serious sins, yet the Catholic Church separates sin into two categories: mortal (serious) and venial (secondary) sins. They consider the serious sins as those stated in the Ten Commandments, including some man-made church laws. However, the secondary sins, which are just as damaging in God's eyes, will hinder the chances for eternal life just as readily as the so-called serious sins if **never** confessed or repented. Holding on to just one ongoing sin (never letting go) could keep us from the Kingdom of Heaven. **True Christians would never jeopardize their salvation by having one ongoing sin that is *never* confessed and repented.**

> *"Those whose steps are guided by the Lord; whose way God approves may stumble, but they will never fall, for the Lord holds their hand." (Psalm 37:23–24)*

Something as ordinary as **carrying back negative tales** or **gossiping** is a hindrance to society and can cause much unhappiness. Rid yourself of all **malice, deceit, hypocrisy, conceit, cursing** and **envy**. Then there are the ADDICTIONS of **drugs, alcohol, gambling, gluttony, pornography, sexual immorality** and other **abuses**. Nor should there be any **foolish talk** or **coarse joking and obscenity**.

When it comes to the children, the Lord's heart is very heavy when they are mistreated. He wants them to have proper discipline and a "tough love" from the parents or caregivers, but is angry at **abusive, uncaring, unfair** and **unloving** parents. The beginning of a child's life plays such a big role in what he or she will be as an adult.

Rid yourself of **impatience, fits of rage, hurtful jealousy, unkindness** and **unfairness**, along with **keeping a record of wrongdoings, selfishness, false pride, greed** and **idolatry** (those who practice magic arts), as well as **lust** and **unreasoning desires**.

Unfortunately, too many people feel that the quote from the Old Testament, *"An eye for eye and tooth for tooth"* means God accepts personal revenge or vigilante situations. This is *not* true. We should *not* take the law into our own hands unless it is to protect ourselves and loved ones. God is love, hence evil for evil is *not* His wish. We must pray for our enemies and let the laws of the land dispense justice.

> *"Do not repay evil with evil or insult with insult, but with blessing." (1 Peter 3:8)*

Laws are *not* made for the righteous, but for lawbreakers and rebels, the **ungodly** and **sinful**, the **unholy** and **irreligious**, for **murderers, adulterers** and **perverts, slave traders, liars, thieves** and **perjurers**.

Bigotry and **prejudice** are very popular sins but are oftentimes considered a personal feeling and, since there could be no negative action involved, many feel these are *not* sins. The Lord wants us to be in control of our unholy thoughts, and we should pray to the Lord to keep our minds pure and try to be fair.

And then there are the African-Americans who too often are discriminated against.[27] There are altogether too many racists who are unfair in judging these people. They are human beings like everyone else whose odds have been clearly stacked against them. We often hear, *"I was poor and grew out of it. Why can't they?"* Most people do *not* understand the plight of the African-Americans, and because of their color, they are often suppressed even today. They have been severely wounded in the African-American world and have been in the prison of negativity for too long. The fact that they have been downtrodden, poverty stricken and abused, it is no wonder so many become a problem to society. God has touched them in a special way, for with all their despair and racial discrimination, multitudes have survived in the name of the Lord. Their praise in song is exhilarating, their belief is evident.

> *"Sing praise, play music; Proclaim all His wondrous deeds!" (Psalm 105:2)*

However, bigotry and prejudice are sins. All nationalities may harbor those who are lazy, unholy, and a hindrance to society, but we should have compassion for everyone. **Racism doesn't just occur to African-Americans. All colors and creeds should be treated equally.** Traveling the road of cultural differences can be bumpy. We tend to accept what we like and reject what we don't about each other's culture. It requires that we release something of ourselves to make room for the new.

Unforgiveness is a prevalent and damaging sin. Unfortunately, this sin exists even among Christians. We should get rid of all **bitterness, rage, anger, brawling** and **slander**, along with every form of **malice**.

> *"Be kind and compassionate with one another, forgiving each other just as in Christ God forgave you."* *(Ephesians 4:31)*

Masturbation, as Webster's New Collegiate Dictionary (1977) defines it, *"is to manipulate one's own genitals or the genitals of another for sexual gratification."* This is a very hush-hush, sensitive, and puzzling subject. Many a young man was told by his confessor (or parents) that he would have serious consequences if this act was continued. Hence, in many cases damaging guilt feelings were embedded. Why does God give very young, innocent children this sensation if it is so wrong? Like some other natural actions or feelings, **when out of control, carried to an abnormal degree, or when it becomes a disturbing preoccupation, it is definitely a sin.** Masturbation could also be beneficial in a marital situation when one spouse, for various reasons, is unable to come into union with his or her mate. **We should *never* choose a way of life in which there is no control. We can only strive to change controlling conditions**.

Divorce. *"I tell you that anyone who divorces his spouse (except for marital unfaithfulness) and marries another commits adultery."* (Matthew 5:32)

God hates divorce, but this is *not* the "unpardonable sin" as many believe it to be. However, it is a sin, and like all other sins, it can be forgiven by the Lord when sincerely confessed and repented. Being **truly** remorseful and compassionate is essential in regard to all the pain that erupted from this unholy situation. **If anger and bitterness continue to prevail, then the sin of divorce remains. We must truly forgive others in order to gain forgiveness from the Lord.** Involved parties should treat each other civilly and with understanding. All children like to see their parents in harmony with one another, more so the children of divorced parents. Maintaining a holy attitude is the key to the Lord's absolution.

Of course, there are legitimate grounds for divorce. When one spouse is being emotionally or physically abused, this is intolerable. You don't have to submit to someone who is battering you or forcing you to do indecent things. The other ground for divorce is adultery. Beyond abuse and adultery, there are no other grounds for a Christian to divorce another Christian.

Temptation, in itself, is *not* a sin. Prayer is the first remedy for temptation. Temptation is usually caused by the devil, the enemy of truth. He disturbs followers of Christ because he hates and fears their way of life. He does *not* bother habitual sinners in this way because he has already captured them. If you are tempted in any manner, do *not* become anxious and troubled. Do *not* let doubts rob you of your peace. Simply put your trust in God, and the enemy will be put to flight. Temptation begins with a thought, then there is a fantasy, then there's a desire to make a choice, and the choice should be of God and *not* of Satan. However, if you choose Satan's way, then temptation turns into a sin.

Running from temptation is usually *not* the answer—we should face our demons and correct them in a holy way.

> *"Watch and pray so that you will not fall into temptation. The Spirit is willing but the body is weak." (Matthew 26:41)*

Homosexuality. This condition is highly misunderstood as it entails ungodly ways regarding sexual gratification. Most people with this affliction are usually confused and unhappy with their abnormal feelings regarding their sexual preference. **However, these feelings are a sin only when acted upon.** Many, as we know, are fighting for their "rights" to be recognized as normal.

There is no scientific proof, yet, that this condition could possibly stem from an inborn trait (a matter of a defective gene). However, through the use of exciting new engineering techniques, researchers are coming ever closer to being able to correct defective genes before a baby is born. There are two choices that can be made—one is to go along with the Gay Movement (consistently sinning); the other is to become celibate, which is an extreme sacrifice. Confessing, repenting and **striving** never to sin again are very difficult tasks and this is what has to be done in order to be in God's favor. **There is an enormous difference between being a celibate homosexual and being a practicing one.** In my opinion, Catholic celibate homosexuals should be able to attain the same church positions as celibate heterosexuals.

Then there are the bisexuals who can perform with the opposite sex, but in reality prefer their own gender. Many get married and even have children, often keeping their sexual preference a secret. There is usually discord in these marriages.

Another group is those who were sexually abused as children and grew up extremely confused as to their sexual desires. Psychiatric help is very often needed in these cases. **However, with the power of Jesus Christ, they can change.**

There are reported incidents where some people have actually made a positive turnabout in their "gay" lifestyle due to counseling and prayers. It is felt that this sparse group actually experienced Divine Intervention. **And what is Divine Intervention? It is when God (often through His angels) compels or prevents an action—or alters a condition.**

> *"Do not lie with a man as one lies with a woman, that is detestable." (Leviticus 18:22)*

Feelings are neither right nor wrong, it is the "action" that counts. **However, if sinful feelings are dwelled upon with continued fantasy and desire, this may be considered a sin.** Each person is responsible for their own actions and by keeping close to God's "will" you will strive to keep from falling into Satan's trap, hence, putting to death whatever belongs to your sinful, carnal nature.

> *"For the wages of sin is death, but the gift of God is eternal life in Christ Jesus our Lord." (Romans 6:23)*

The Unpardonable Sin is "hate" and "vengeance" toward the Holy Spirit. This is the sin God hates the most and will *never* forgive these Satanic worshipers who are definitely slated for the fires of hell.[28]

> *"He who conceals his sins does not prosper, but whoever confesses (to Jesus) and renounces them finds mercy." (Proverb 28:13)*

YIELDING TO SIN AND TEMPTATION DOES *NOT* FIT WHO YOU ARE IN CHRIST.

"And so I tell you, every sin and blasphemy against the Spirit will NOT be forgiven. Anyone who speaks a word against the Son of Man, will be forgiven, but anyone who speaks against the Holy Spirit will NOT be forgiven either in this age or the age to come." (Matthew 12:31–32)

"You have taken off your old self with its practices and have put on the new self, which is being renewed in knowledge in the image of its creator." (Colossians 3:9–10)

---

[27] Those who are of a paler shade of black usually have a better chance of being accepted. In other words, to most, the more they resemble "white" in color and features, the more of a chance they have to succeed. This is not a fair situation. However, as a nation, we have improved somewhat in this area.

[28] Reference to sins: Col. 3:5–9; 1-Cor. 6:18; Eph. 4:31; Eph. 5:3–4, Luke 18:20; Mk. 14:57; Mt. 5:21; Mt. 5:27; Mt. 6:15; Mt. 15:19–20.

After the Ascension

PRISONERS OF CHILDHOOD

(Grow Up In Christ)

We are products of our past, but we don't have to be prisoners of our past. It is no secret that parents have the power to deform the emotional life of their children. Parental contempt and lack of respect can easily damage a child's personality. However, most people, with good intent and love, try to provide healthy environments for their children. **But too often parents are unaware of the damage they could be doing.**

Consequently, there are too many who are seriously effected by their upbringing, especially where incest, violence and perversion are practiced. These people have a legitimate reason for perhaps *not* rising above their circumstances and for experiencing special problems that can probably only be solved with psychiatric treatment or counseling. Christians know that Jesus is the ultimate healer and that faith and prayers are beneficial for all needs.

But for those poor souls who never forgive their parents for not showing love, this is a sign of serious immaturity. If only they could realize that most parents do (and did) the best that they know (and knew) how. Remember, they had parents too, and sometimes it's difficult to show love if one hasn't been shown love in the earlier years.

To FORGIVE is the secret and to understand that their parents had "hang-ups" too. Most parental faults probably came from unaware incompetence. Many basically good people were most likely in the dark as to handling their children differently than the way they were handled or raised. The level of intelligence in a person has nothing do to with it. It's a case of the level of compassion and maturity.

THERE'S A DIFFERENCE BETWEEN TOUGH LOVE AND UNFAIR PUNISHMENT.

> *"Fathers, do not provoke or irritate or fret your children lest they become discouraged and sullen and morose and feel inferior and frustrated. Do not break their spirit." (Colossians 3:21)*

> *"There are those who curse their fathers and do not bless their mothers; those who are pure in their own eyes and yet are not cleansed of their filth." (Proverbs 30:11–12)*

> *"Remember not the sins of my youth and my rebellious ways; according to your love remember me, for you are good, O Lord." (Psalm 25:7)*

After the Ascension

A WAKE-UP CALL

(And the Beat Goes On)

God's greatest wish is for all to be saved. Unless souls are saved, nothing is saved. Nothing will happen in the external world that has *not* first happened within a soul.

Again, becoming Born Again (or Saved) is governed by the spirit of the individual. It is *not* an unholy cult; it is *not* a strange religion. Out of the **searching**, out of the **hunger**, out of the **thirst** for salvation comes the commitment of Jesus—accepting Him as our Lord and Savior. There should be a presence of a burning desire to please Him. And it is written (Bible) that the only way to get to the Kingdom of Heaven is through Jesus, Son of God. He is our only intercessor and we must put aside all our bad habits, sinful ways, other idols and have a clean conscience before God in order to gain everlasting life in Heaven.

When this glorious acceptance of Jesus occurs, you have come out of the darkness and into the light (truth). **He then becomes the light of your life, a light that starts with a flicker and gradually grows and grows into a flame, whereby becoming completely on fire for the Lord.** In return for your gift to Him (accepting Him fully in your life), His gift to you is the anointment of becoming baptized through the Holy Spirit. It must be mentioned again that the gift of love is always more important than the gift of tongues or any other spiritual gift.

In regard to becoming a true Christian, there are true conversions and false conversions. Making the initial promise and then backsliding extensively is *not* our Lord's way. He is very unhappy with His fallen flock. His way is *not* to become "lax" in following Him. Not only must we sincerely try to be the best Christian possible (by example), but we should spread the word in any Christian way that we can. We should also *not* allow ourselves to come across as a "flake," but we should always speak up in the name of Jesus, lifting Him up to make Him visible to the world. Too often we fail Him in doing this.

There will be times when we take a stand for righteousness and we may be rejected. **BEING RIGHTEOUS DOES NOT MEAN ALWAYS BEING RIGHT. It means those who live righteously strive to act in accord with divine and moral law and to be free from sin.** They know by the word they are the righteousness of God in Christ and that they are masters over circumstances and demons. It is the word of righteousness that sets us free, leads us out of Satan's dominion into the liberty and freedom to grow into a spiritual life in Christ.

> IF GOD ONLY USED PERFECT PEOPLE,
> NOTHING WOULD EVERY GET DONE.

> *"By waiting and by calm you shall be saved,*
> *in quiet and in trust your strength lies . . ."*
> *(Isaiah 30:15)*

> *"The lips of the righteous know what is fitting, but*
> *the mouth of the wicked only what is perverse."*
> *(Proverbs 10:32)*

After the Ascension

HOW COULD WE

*How could we appreciate the Silence
If we never heard the Noise*

*How could we understand Solitude
If we never experienced Loneliness*

*How could we recognize Patience
If we never encountered Anger*

*How could we be aware of Beauty
If Ugliness was extinct*

*How could we appreciate Peace
If we never experienced Wartime*

*How could we know we were Fortunate
If the Unfortunate didn't exist*

And most importantly

*How could we know how to Love
If we were never Loved*

*However, we should remember
There's always GOD to love us
And for us to love His Son
Is a big spiritual plus.*

M. Grace Ferri

M. GRACE FERRI

TURN YOUR LIFE AROUND

Start by truly forgiving
    and turn your life around,

Firstly, by forgiving unto "yourself"
    then your enemies who let you down.

Plant a seed of faith in the Lord
    and watch how you will grow,

To heights so rewarding
    that only you will know.

The beautiful feelings of serenity
    that will surely come your way,

When you walk in HIS path
    day by day.

Love should always prevail
    the kind that is very "giving,"

Not mainly material things,
    more so, HIS virtues should we be exhibiting.

And by combining the great forces of loving JESUS,
    confessing, repenting, praying and forgiving
    (seventy times seven)[29],

Only then can the victory be won,
    which is the Kingdom of Heaven.

                                M. Grace Ferri

---

[29]"Seven" is the most commonly used number in the Bible.

After the Ascension

LET "HIM" IN

All we need is a little bit of light to get us going
    In order to start the spiritual process of growing.

For those who do not live for Heaven are the fools
    And as to whom we should glorify
    there should be no duels.

For the God of the Heavens should always win out
    And then the god of earth (Satan) will really pout.

It is not easy to be obedient to the Lord up above
    But the results will be ever so rewarding
    when we live in complete love.

For it is love alone in the long run
    that will be the real test.
And our level of love will surely determine
    our last place of rest.

But until we search for a deeper understanding
    of Christ in our lives.
Your light may sadly flicker forever without ever
    becoming the big flame that lights up HIS life.

                                            M. Grace Ferri

M. GRACE FERRI

THE FOLLOWING ESSAYS
INCLUDE SOME OF THE HIGHLIGHTS
IN THE LIFE OF CHRIST

After the Ascension

GOD SENT US A SAVIOR

If our greatest need had been information
God would have sent us an educator

If our greatest need had been technology
God would have sent us a scientist

If our greatest need had been money
God would have sent us an economist

If our greatest need had been pleasure
God would have sent us an entertainer

But our greatest need was forgiveness
So God sent us a Savior[30]

(Author Unknown)

---

[30] Our greatest need was "forgiveness," but it's evident that Jesus also covered the other needs mentioned.

MARY WAS CHOSEN

The Virgin Mary was chosen from all time to have the greatest privilege a creature could enjoy. The second person of the Trinity would take a body and soul like ours, be conceived in Mary's womb and be born of her so that she would be the Mother of Jesus.[31] At God's appointed time, the Angel Gabriel entered Mary's home and announced to her God's plan. At that time, she was betrothed to a countryman named Joseph. The humble girl was puzzled and troubled by the words of the Angel Gabriel, but the angel explained the Divine Plan which insured that she would be the Mother of the Anointed One yet remain a virgin. The conception would take place through the Holy Spirit (Holy Ghost).[32]

After her three month stay with Elizabeth, mother-to-be of John the Baptist, Mary returned home in preparation for the **greatest birth of all time**. Joseph had to learn of her miraculous conception. Mary had full confidence that God would settle Joseph's doubts by revealing to him her exalted privilege, which God did through a dream.

> *"When Joseph awoke, he did what the Angel of the Lord had commanded him and took Mary home as his wife,* **but he had no union with her until she gave birth to a son and he gave Him the name of Jesus.***" (Matthew 1:25)*

Mary and Joseph were married in a simple Jewish ceremony and then they began their married life, a model of dedication and simplicity. Jesus was born in the surroundings of poverty. God chose a borrowed stable for His Son's birth and chose a borrowed grave for His death. Consistently, our Lord would teach by word and example the necessity of self-denial.

Regarding the apparitions of the Blessed Mary, it has been reported repeatedly that **all she wants is for us to follow her Son**. She wants us to direct our thoughts, desires and actions as her Son desires. She doesn't want us to forsake her Beloved Son Jesus Christ by putting her first.

The honor we can pay our Blessed Mother is to imitate her virtues in our daily life, but the greatest honor is to follow her Son, our Lord and Savior, for He alone is the Truth and the Way and the Life.

> *". . . Mary was pledged to be married to Joseph, but **before they came together**, she was found to be with child through the Holy Spirit." (Matthew 1:18)*

> *"For God so loved the world that He gave His only Son, that whoever believes in Him should not perish but have eternal life." (John 3:16)*

Jesus' Mother and Brothers

> *"Then Jesus' **Mother**[33] **and brothers** arrived. Standing outside, they sent someone in to call on them. A crowd was sitting around Him, and they told Him, '**Your Mother and brothers are outside looking for you.**' 'Who are my Mother and Brothers?' he asked. Then He looked at those seated in a circle around Him and said, 'Here are my Mother and my brothers! Whoever does*

God's will is my brother and sister and Mother.'"
(Mark 3:31–35)

---

[31] The Jewish Christians identify Jesus as a descendent of David and thus, the Messiah, the true heir of David's Kingdom. Their reference to the genealogy of Jesus is in Matthew 1:1–17.

[32] And then there are those Jewish people who believe that Christ has yet to come.

[33] Most Catholics believe that our Blessed Mother remained a virgin forever. The quotes from the Bible (Matthew 1:18, 25 and Mark 3:31–35) pose doubts as to the validity of the Catholic rendition regarding this matter.

BAPTISM

(With Water and the Holy Spirit)

Predicted upon faith and repentance, baptism is an outward sign of our inward commitment. It represents a new beginning. The "old" person, with all of his sinful past, is symbolically buried and a new creation comes forth. The waters of baptism symbolize the fact that we are washed clean inwardly through the Holy Spirit.

Many of us were baptized as a baby with a sprinkling of water on our head. When we grew older, this was explained to us by the church that this act was done to cleanse us of original sin handed down from Adam and Eve in the Garden of Eden. This is where they disregarded God's perfect plan for them and surrendered to the devil.

As time went on and other Christians were talking about becoming Born Again by being baptized with immersion in water, it was then that certain Christian denominations began to preach that the act performed to a Christian infant was a "Born Again" experience. **A baby, who has no sins, knows nothing about "believing," being "saved" or confessing and repenting.** By nature, a baby is selfish and demanding. An infant is incapable of thirsting for the "Love of Jesus." All that infants thirst for is milk and comforting nurturing. It is just impossible for a baby to grasp the true meaning of baptism by water or being baptized with the Holy Spirit. Therefore, the belief that the sprinkling of water (on an infant) is null and void as far as being

"Born Again" is concerned. Unfortunately, many Christians still believe they were Born Again when sprinkled as a baby.

Baptism usually represents the beginning of the conversion process and is *not* something we can enter into lightly. Before being baptized with immersion in water, we should be of an age to understand why Jesus died on the cross for us and all mankind. We should know how to confess and repent our sins and realize that we must strive to make a positive spiritual change in our way of life. We also should surrender our life to Jesus, Son of God, and only then are we renewed in the Spirit. **Nevertheless, multitudes of Christians who were baptized without full immersion in water (conversion with the grace of God) became baptized in the Holy Spirit, often with evidence of speaking in tongues.**

It is evident that the light sprinkling of water is *not* the way God intended us to be baptized. For wasn't Jesus baptized in the River Jordan, with immersion, by John the Baptist? Jesus, of course, was without sin, but He insisted that John baptize Him. John had baptized many before Jesus emerged from His hidden life. After the baptism of Jesus, when He stepped from the water, the Holy Spirit descended on Jesus in the form of a dove, and a voice from Heaven said, *"This is my beloved Son whom I love; with him I am well pleased."* Matthew 3:17(NIV). This was the first time the Heavenly Father, His only begotten Son and the Holy Spirit were present at the same time.

After this "happening," Jesus then appointed the disciples to do the baptizing (in the same manner He had been baptized) to those who wanted to be cleansed of their sins and follow

God's will. The complete immersion signifies washing away all sins and then bringing them up from the water to a new life in Jesus.[34] However, there are some who are immersed in water and do *not* fully experience a new life in Jesus. These people need to re-evaluate their spiritual life and pray for salvation through the grace of God.

CHRISTIANS SHOULD BE BAPTIZED BY TOTAL IMMERSION BECAUSE WATER REPRESENTS BOTH LIFE AND DEATH, WHEREBY MAKING THIS ACT "DEATH TO SIN" AND "LIFE TO CHRIST." ACTUALLY, THIS SHOULD NOT OCCUR BEFORE THE AGE OF REASONING.

> *"Whomever believes and is baptized will be saved, but whoever does not believe will be condemned." (Mark 16:16)*

> *"John baptized with water but you will be baptized with the Holy Spirit." (Acts 11:16)*

---

[34] As an infant, I was baptized in the Catholic Church with only the sprinkling of water. However, as an **adult** I was baptized in the Holy Spirit, without complete immersion, evidenced by speaking in tongues.

M. Grace Ferri

THE SERMON ON THE MOUNT
(Beatitudes)

POWERFUL WORDS BY JESUS TO HIS DISCIPLES

"Blessed are the poor in spirit, for theirs is the kingdom of heaven."

Our experience of life in Christ begins as we recognize our need. We cannot turn to our material successes, our personal accomplishments, or our spiritual piety. The Gospel proclaims that this recognition can lead us through the doorway to blessedness, where joy and suffering can exist simultaneously.

"Blessed are those who mourn, for they will be comforted."

Normally we view grief and joy as opposites, yet in the Gospel, grief is the doorway to the house of joy. Grieving proclaims that life is not as it should be. The Lord of the kingdom weeps—Jesus wept over Lazarus' death and the deadness of Jerusalem. God is able to comfort us in our mourning because he has shared in our grief.

"Blessed are the meek, for they will inherit the earth."

Meekness is one of the most misunderstood moral qualities. In our society, a meek person is a spineless weakling. Actually, Jesus used a word that expresses the relinquishment of all illusion of control. Those who know their utter dependence on

God, and are trained to trust God in all things, know that they have nothing to lose.

"Blessed are those who hunger and thirst for righteousness, for they will be filled."

Life in the kingdom is described as a banquet, a perpetual feast to which all are welcome but to which only those who know their hunger come. The Gospel promises that God feeds those who hunger for righteousness—the holiness and justice that will cure the suffering of our world.

"Blessed are the merciful, for thy will be shown mercy."

To be merciful is to be patiently forgiving toward others. Mercy hurts. But in being merciful, we celebrate God's grace in overcoming all offense and reconciling us in Jesus Christ.

"Blessed are the pure in heart, for they will see God."

Only when we live with nothing to hide can we experience blessedness. We need no longer linger in the darkness, for we have come completely into the light. We are set free to stand joyously before God when we know that in mercy, he has cleansed our shameful sin with the goodness of Christ.

"Blessed are the peacemakers, for they will be called sons of God."

The word for peace, "eirene," refers to weaving back together a torn garment. The shattered fabric of our lives is rewoven into a seamless whole in Christ, such that through the Spirit, we are one body. Having experienced this peace, we desire passionately that others find it, too.

"Blessed are those who are persecuted because of righteousness, for theirs is the kingdom of heaven."

To follow Jesus is to be in conflict with the values of this world. It is to be persecuted. But this suffering is only the temporary consequence of the dissonance that exists between the kingdoms of light and darkness. The light has triumphed. No opposition can succeed in blocking our path into the kingdom of God.

"Blessed are you when people insult you, persecute you and falsely say all kinds of evil against you because of me."

Rejoice and be glad, because great is your reward in heaven, for in the same way they persecuted the prophets who were before you.

Beatitudes (Matthew 5:3–12)[35]
Explanations of Beatitudes are from *World Vision Magazine*

---

[35]Explanations of Beatitudes taken from World Vision Magazine, Volume 8, Number 2. Copyright 2004.

After the Ascension

THE TRANSFIGURATION

(This Incident "Blew Their Minds")

Jesus temporarily appears in a new exalting, glorifying and spiritual way. The story about the transformed Jesus seen by Peter, James and John after Jesus had led them up a high mountain is *not* as well known as the other stories in the Bible.

Jesus was transfigured before them. His face shone like the sun and His clothes became as white as the light. Just then there appeared before them Moses and Elijah talking with Jesus. Peter offered to put up three shelters; one for Jesus, one for Moses and one for Elijah. While Peter was still speaking, a bright cloud enveloped them and a voice from the cloud said:

> *"This is My Son, whom I love; with Him I am well pleased. Listen to Him." (Matthew 17:5)(NIV)*

When the disciples heard this, they fell face down to the ground terrified, but Jesus came and touched them and told them to get up and *not* be afraid. When they looked up, they saw no one but Jesus. As they were coming down the mountain, Jesus instructed them *not* to tell anyone what they had seen until the Son of Man (Jesus) had been raised from the dead.

The disciples asked Jesus, *"Why do the teachers of law say that Elijah must come first?"* Jesus replied:

> *"To be sure, Elijah comes and will restore all things. But I tell you, Elijah has already come and they did not recognize him, but have done everything they wished in the same way the Son of*

Man is going to suffer at their hands." (Matthew 17:10–12)

Then the disciples understood. He was talking to them about John the Baptist.

What is the true message of this story? Could it be that God wanted to make sure the three disciples were completely assured that Jesus was definitely who He said He was, whereby taking all doubts away from them? They were told *not* to say anything to anyone until the Son of Man was raised from the dead. Hence, the other nine disciples were never completely reassured as these three. He evidently wanted the others to continue on "faith" alone until the given time.[36]

> *"I tell you the truth, whoever hears my words and believes him who sent me has eternal life and will not be condemned; he has crossed over from death to life." (John 5:24)*

About Elijah:

Prophet and man of God. Predicted famine in Israel. Raised Sidonian widow's son. Ran from Jezebel. Defeated prophets of Baal at Carmel. Prophesied death of Azariah, King of Samaria. Taken to Heaven in a whirlwind. Succeeded by Elisha, prophet successor to Elijah. (2 Kings 1:1-17; 2:1-15)

About John The Baptist:

Son of Zechariah and Elizabeth (cousin to Mary, Mother of Christ). Called the Baptist. Witness to Jesus. Baptized Jesus in the River Jordan. Was beheaded by Herod while he was in prison. (For more on John the Baptist, read Matthew 11:1–15; 14:1–12)

---

[36] August 6th is observed as a Christian feast in commemoration of the transfiguration of Christ on a mountaintop with three disciples looking on.

M. Grace Ferri

THE LAST SUPPER

THE TWELVE APOSTLES

*SIMON, WHOM JESUS CALLED PETER,
HIS BROTHER ANDREW, JAMES, JOHN, PHILLIP,
BARTHOLOMEW, MATTHEW, THOMAS, JAMES,
SIMON, JUDAS, SON OF JAMES, AND
JUDAS ISCARIOT WHO BECAME A TRAITOR.*

After the Ascension

THE LAST SUPPER

A council composed of chief priests, scribes and elders, having now finally rejected Jesus, met that night in the house of Caiaphas. Christ's popularity constrained them to take Him secretly. Thus, did Judas, the traitor, play into their hands by his offer to betray the Master. They agreed to pay him thirty shekels (about seventeen dollars) for his treachery.

Wednesday passed without incident. Early Thursday morning, the day of Pasch, Jesus sent Peter and John to Jerusalem to find a room and prepare for the Paschal meal where Jesus, with the others, joined them in the evening. Before the supper the Master set them an example of humility by washing the feet of each.

When the meal was over, our Lord informed them that He knew that one of them would betray Him. Stunned by this news, each one frantically blurred out, *"Is it I, Lord?"* Judas, sitting near, attempting a pathetic bluff, asked the same question. Our Lord replied quietly, *"Thou hast said it."* Rejecting the Master's offer of repentance, Judas hurried out into the night.[37]

Then Jesus fulfilled His promise to give His flesh and blood as our food and drink. He blessed and broke bread and giving it to them bade them eat it saying, *"This is my body."* Then He took the cup and giving thanks, gave it to them with the words, *"Drink ye all of this for this is my blood of the New Testament which is shed for many for the remission of sins."* In these words Our Lord linked forever the ceremony of the Last Supper with His glorious sacrifice on Calvary.

The main theme of the Catholic daily mass is based on the

words of Christ at the Last Supper regarding His body and blood. A wafer (depicting His body) is dispensed to the parishioners who have confessed and repented of all their sins. Previous to accepting the "body of Christ," they should promise the Lord that they will **strive** never to sin again, whereby "receiving" with a completely cleansed and purified heart. It is quite possible that there are many who just "receive" without knowing the truths associated with this Holy procedure. Unfortunately, many may think that by just partaking of this wafer and faithfully attending Mass they assuredly will be destined for the Kingdom of Heaven. Sadly, this is erroneous thinking. **True Christians know the only guarantee to the Kingdom of Heaven is to become a Born Again Christian.** (Refer to essay entitled *"Clarification of Born Again or Saved."*)

> *"I tell you, I will not drink of this fruit of the vine from now on until that day when I drink it anew with you in my Father's kingdom"*
> *(Matthew 26:29)*

---

[37] For more information about Judas, who hangs himself after redemption, refer to Matt. 26:14–15, Matt. 27:1–10. Judas was replaced by Thaddeus.

After the Ascension

AGONY IN THE GARDEN

After the Last Supper, there was Jesus' agony in the garden at Mount Olivet where He was horrified in His human nature at the picture of His coming sufferings. A sickening mixture of sorrow, fright, disgust, and frustration flooded His soul. He cried out to His Father for relief, but immediately qualified His prayer with submission, *"Thy will be done."* So intense was the agony that blood oozed forth from the pores of His Body and trickled to the ground. Hence, Jesus suffered immensely even before the "Cross."

FREEDOM IS YOURS
WHEN YOU CLAIM
YOUR TRUE POSITION IN CHRIST—
SAVED, SEALED, AND SANCTIFIED BY GOD.

"Whoever acknowledges me before men, I will also acknowledge him before my Father in heaven. But whoever disowns me before men, I will disown him before my Father in heaven." (Matthew 10:32–33)

THE CROSS OF CHRIST

FROM THE CROSS, JESUS SPOKE THE MOST MATURE WORDS EVER SPOKEN:

"Father, forgive them for they do not know what they are doing." (Luke 23:34)

After the Ascension

THE CROSS

(Faith In All Its Glory)

Jesus came to us as the Lamb of God, holy and without sin. He shed His blood for the atonement of sins. There is no stronger message than the message of God's forgiveness and grace. Each one of us at some point in life will be confronted with the message of the Cross of Christ. There is no escaping it.

Jesus' life and death were the satisfaction of God's plan to eradicate once and for all the penalty of mankind's sin. When you place your trust in Christ as your Savior, God forgives all your sins: past, present and future. We should celebrate daily what God did for us on the Cross; for it is there that He gave all of Himself so that we might have eternal life.

Jesus was born to die on the Cross. The crucifixion of God's Son is sufficient payment for mankind's sin, and the resurrection is God's stamp of approval for the penalty payment. Also, take away the resurrection of Christ and you reduce Christianity to the level of the ethnic religions. Satan has long attempted to defame and destroy its message, the message of salvation and eternal hope. Jesus' death and resurrection, however, brought tremendous hope and eternal freedom.

Incorrectly perceived by many, the events of the cross were considered just a severe punishment by Pontius Pilate due to the fact that Jesus claimed to be the Son of God and King of the Jews. As Christians, we know it was more than that. If Jesus had denied being the Son of God, He would have been set free.

But Jesus, always being obedient to God His Father, told the truth and suffered the consequences. **The events of the cross are the greatest contribution to Christianity the world will ever know.**

Before Jesus was nailed to the Cross, He was severely **SCOURGED.** His beard was plucked from His face and His skin was pulled away from His bones. A wreath of thorns was put on His head that pierced into His skull. Finally, after **several** forms of humiliating torture, Jesus became unrecognizable. He was then nailed to the cross and hung there for six hours in pain and agony. Then He died to live again with His Father in the Kingdom of Heaven. The price had been paid. The sacrifice for human sin had been fulfilled, thus, the reconciliation of Man to God came about through the sacrificial death of our beloved Jesus Christ.

Jesus knew this terrible ordeal would have to happen in order that people could be set free from their sins. We may have been freed from the slavery of sins, but only to become slaves of righteousness so we may have eternal life. He was the bearer of the world's sins and because of His love for us He suffered this horrible death on the cross.

> *Old Convenant: "Anyone who rejected the law of Moses died without mercy on the testimony of two or three witnesses." (Hebrews 10:28)*

> *" . . . He sets aside the first (Old Covenant) to establish the second (New Covenant) and by that we have been made holy through the sacrifice of the body of Jesus Christ once for all." (Hebrews 10:9–10)*

After the Ascension

Now with this new covenant, the sinners can confess, repent, and ask for forgiveness. From the Cross he also forgave the souls of the sinners who were in Hades.

If it was *not* for the events of the cross, all sinners would have been doomed for Hades with no life ever after. It is unfortunate that so many people do *not* take advantage of this gift of salvation that the Lord gave us from the cross. The cross is a symbol of God's supreme love, sacrifice and forgiveness. In far too many cases, the cross that is now embraced by our world is *not* the cross of Jesus Christ. It is a cross that is worn without conviction or sincerity.[38]

> *"But he was pierced for our transgressions, he was crushed for our iniquities; the punishment that brought us peace was upon him, and by his wounds we are healed." (Isaiah 53:5)*

---

[38] During the days of Christian persecution, they had to disguise the cross and one of the most common disguises was an anchor.

M. Grace Ferri

WHO KILLED JESUS?

(A Personal Reflection)

Some blame the Jews and some blame the Romans for the crucifixion of Jesus; it was neither. Jesus was born to die on the Cross for the forgiveness of sins. His life and death were prophesied in the Old Testament. He came to us as a Lamb of God, holy and without sin. His life and death were the satisfaction of **God's plan** to eradicate, once and for all, the penalty of mankind's sin. God sacrificed His Son so we might have eternal life. No gift has been greater than the gift Jesus has given to us. So who killed Jesus? In reality, God His Father was responsible for the death of His son for reasons mentioned above.

HIS LIFE CHANGED HISTORY
HIS DEATH CHANGED ETERNITY

"Yet it was the Lord's will to crush him and cause him to suffer, and through the Lord makes his life a guilt offering he will see his off spring and prolong his days, and the will of the Lord will prosper in his hand." (Isaiah 53:10)

"In him we have redemption through his blood, the forgiveness of sins, in accordance with the riches of God's grace that he lavished on us with all wisdom and understanding." (Ephesians 1:7)

After the Ascension

THE RESURRECTION

(The Greatest Miracle of All Time)

A group of women, led by Mary Magdalene, discovered the empty tomb very early in the morning that Sunday over 2,000 years ago. They had been close to Jesus and they went to the tomb to anoint the body of Jesus with special burial spices. At first they saw the guards on the ground in a coma-like state. When they saw the stone rolled away and with no body, they were very astonished. Then, to add to their shock, two shining angels appeared and said:

> *"Why do you seek the living One among the dead? He is not here, but He has risen." (Luke 24:5–6)*

The women believed what the angels said, as they remembered Jesus telling them that He would rise again. After Mary Magdalene fled to bear word to Peter and John, Peter boldly went in first and saw the bandages and shroud carefully folded. Then John came in and looked around the empty tomb. In the Word of Scripture, *"He saw and believed."*

Of course, many rumors were circulating and some said it was all a hoax. But anyone who heard the news or saw Him face to face had to make the decision. Did they believe it was really Jesus? Either Jesus is who He said He is, the living Son of God, or He is the worst liar or the craziest man who ever lived. This may sound harsh, but the choices are really that simple.

The very first miracle was performed at the wedding at Cana when they ran out of wine and Jesus turned urns of water into wine at His Mother's request. **But the greatest miracle of**

all time comes from the empty tomb where Jesus rose from the dead. Jesus then appeared to many, at different times, before He went back to Heaven to sit at the right hand of the Father.

> LIFE WITH CHRIST IS AN ENDLESS HOPE
> LIFE WITHOUT CHRIST IS A HOPELESS END.

> *"Jesus said unto her (Martha[39]),* ***I am the resurrection, and the life. He who believes in me will live, even though he dies, and whoever lives and believes in me will never die."*** *(Matthew 11:25–26)*

> *"The angel said to the women, do not be afraid, for I know that you are looking for Jesus. He is not here; he has risen, just as he said. Come and see the place where he lay." (Matthew 28:5–6)*

---

[39] Martha and Mary were the sisters of Lazarus whom Jesus raised to life four days after he died. Lazarus was Jesus' best friend and due to frequent visits to their house, Jesus became very fond of Martha and Mary.

AFTER THE RESURRECTION
(He Appeared In A Mystical Body)

Jesus did *not* ascend into Heaven immediately after He had risen from the dead, as so many believe. His first appearance was to Mary Magdalene.[40] Initially, she thought He was the gardener and overcome with grief pleaded with Him to tell her where her Master's body had been taken. Then the Savior spoke one word, *"Mary."* It was enough. Her soul overflowing with faith, love and joy, she threw herself at His feet crying out, *"Master."*

Jesus appeared to his disciples and showed them the wounds in His hands and feet to reassure them that He was their Master. Eight days later He returned to rebuke Thomas, who was absent on the previous occasion, for insisting that he must touch the very wounds before believing that He was the Master who had risen from the tomb. That is how the term "Doubting Thomas" originated.

Peter and six other Apostles went to Galilee to fish on the lake. All night they fished, but caught nothing. At dawn they saw a stranger on the shore, and when they pulled near, this man told them to cast their net on the other side of the boat. They did so and immediately made such a catch that they could *not* raise the net. John then recognized Him and cried out to the others, *"It is the Lord."* When Peter heard this, he then jumped into the water and swam the hundred yards to shore. In a happy reunion, they built a fire, made a meal at His invitation and then settled down to hear the Master's word. Jesus took this occasion to continue their training for the commission He had given them to teach all nations, baptizing them in the name of the Father and of the Son and of the Holy Ghost. This training of the Holy Spirit would become complete on Pentecost.

> *"After his suffering, he showed himself to these men and gave many convincing proofs that he was alive. He appeared to them over a period of forty days and spoke about the kingdom of God." (Acts 1:3)*

> *"Jesus came, took the bread and gave it to them, and did the same with the fish. This was now the third time Jesus appeared to His disciples **after** he was raised from the dead." (John 21:13–14)*

---

[40] It is believed by many that Mary Magdalene was the prostitute who was stoned because of her sin. However, approximately 500 A.D. the Catholic Church disproved this theory and came to the conclusion that Mary Magdalene was actually an extremely close friend of Jesus and was **not** the fallen woman that He rescued.

After the Ascension

THE ASCENSION

At the appointed time, our Lord's devoted followers went to Jerusalem and were met there by the Master, who imparted to them His final instruction.[41]

Jesus, whose birth was a miracle, left the earth also in a miraculous fashion. With His Mother, the Apostles, the disciples and the holy women gathered around Him on Mount Olivet, He bade them farewell and as He blessed them, rose in great majesty until a cloud hid Him from sight. Suddenly, two men dressed in white stood beside them and said, "This same Jesus who has been taken from you into heaven, will come back in the same way you have seen Him go into heaven."

> *"He was taken up before their very eyes, and a cloud hid him from their sight." (Acts 1:9)*

---

[41] The Ascension witnessed by many gave Him great power and victory. The **absence** of this witnessed "rising" could have instilled doubts in some believers.

M. Grace Ferri

APOSTLE PAUL
(Saul)

The following italicized portion is from *The Spiritual Journey of St. Paul,* by Lucien Cerfaux.

[42]Paul infused the principles of a higher life. He then created a Christian society, a society of Christian marriages, of regard for chastity, of respect for the personality of every man in Christ and for the value of social laws and civilizations. This is the leaven of purity and truth which will remain and which we shall always hand on to succeeding civilizations on our earth.

The letters of Saint Paul, after twenty centuries, are still so alive for us, still stir us and force us to think. A single line sums them all up: **Faithfulness to the ever-lasting Christ.** *Paul was a man with an outstanding mind, in whom converged the three types of humanity found in the civilized world of his age. He was a thinker, a man of action, an organizer, and a man of feeling. Paul had a mind of exceptional power and was adept at arguing in the manner of the rabbis, yet fundamentally he was an intuitive thinker. He had extraordinary moral and spiritual insight and was able to express what he saw with the confidence of a prophet and with the imaginative resourcefulness of a poet. And all this is harmonized, brought to perfection and fused by the passion of a soul aflame with the most overmastering of fires,* **the fire of the resurrection of Christ.**

The sublime originality of St. Paul will always remain the inspired conception which led him to see everything in and reduce everything to a single focus. **That focus was Christ dead and risen again,** *Christ incorporating the entire company of believers into himself in forming the new man. Paul was a prey to anxiety. He was neither an artist nor a poet, but a man who could handle ideas and crowds, outstanding in his intellectual liveliness and flexibility, keenly sensitive and extremely quick in his reactions. He made it his chief concern not to speak over his listeners' heads. He drew* *his examples from current events, from the humble everyday life of the townspeople, and he was so alive to the feeling of others that when he wrote, he could put himself in his distant correspondents' place.*

The Beginning

Jesus of Nazareth was a child only a few years old when Paul was born at Tarus in Cilicia. It is true that the distance that separates divinity from humanity created an unbridgeable gap between the two Jews. All the same, when the Son of God took flesh, he took everything human on himself **but sin**, *so it may be useful to try and draw a comparison between the two. Such a comparison will help us to grasp the influence of his surroundings on the development of the man and so to understand why it was that Paul, once he had become a rabbi, could NOT but approve the murder of Jesus and become a bitter enemy of His followers.*

Like every Jewish child (in his family and at the Jewish school of Parsus) in the shadow of the synagogue, Paul learned to read Hebrew. At his lesson he would unroll the miniature scrolls of parchment containing passages from Leviticus, the essential book of religious law. Paul's mother could hardly have failed to teach him to pray. The Jew is a man of prayer. It is evident that Paul's Christian formulas, woven as they are out of biblical expressions, testify to the atmosphere of reverence and love of God which surrounded his childhood. The Bible and the whole of Jewish literature are permeated with prayer. It formed the Jew's constant daily companion and kept him, so to say, in the presence of God.

Paul grew up in a spiritual atmosphere of the purest Judaism, with a complete and profound faith. His family belonged to the sect of the Pharisees and that was a fundamental fact in his life. In his speeches and letters, he insisted on the purity of his Jewish ancestry and the strictness of his Judaism. The order in which he sets out his family advantages mounts to a signifi-

cant climax *(Philippians 3:4–5: Galatians 1:13)*. He was distinguished by his membership of the sect of Pharisees, the strictest and the most devoted in whose ranks he had singled himself out by his astonishing spiritual development and by a zeal which did not stop short at persecution.

However, Saul was still breathing out murderous threats against the Lord's disciples. He went to the high priest and asked him for letters to the synagogues in Damascus, so that if he found any there who belonged to the "Way," whether men or women, he might take them as prisoners to Jerusalem.

Meeting With Jesus

The thing happened in a flash; it was violent, but decisive. There was a dazzling light, a look, a few words, Paul later used a magnificent comparison to convey the impression of pure light that had overwhelmed him. He said it was like the first dawn of the world, when at the very beginning of the universe light sprang into existence at the Creator's orders and put the darkness to flight *(2 Corinthians 4:6)*. In fact, a new creation had been ushered in, one far more beautiful than the first. Here we must halt awhile with Paul on the road to Damascus, for what happened to him there was the most important event in the life of the infant church,[43] after the resurrection of Jesus. Paul's message was there in embryo. (Refer to Acts 26:19)

He had seen Jesus of Nazareth, whose crucifixion was still an affair of yesterday, and he had seen him risen and glorified. He had met the Lord face to face, for Christ had appeared to him as convincingly as he had to Peter and the other apostles. All the same, to indicate the unusual character of his vocation and his birth into the life of Christ, Paul was to add: "And last of all, I too saw him, like the last child, that comes to birth unexpectedly." *(1 Corinthians 15:8)* Woe to the man who doubted the reality of the apparition: "Am I not an apostle, have I not seen our Lord Jesus Christ?" *(1 Corinthian 9:1)*

There are the hard facts, then, Jesus of Nazareth showed

himself to Paul. He compelled his recognition by the radiance of his divine presence. In a flash the prostrate Pharisee realized the truth. The road to God which he had been trained to follow since his childhood did not lead to the goal for which he had yearned so passionately. That goal lay outside the Pharisees' ideal. With Christians, he opened the door to the deeper meaning of the experience that God the Father had planned for him; "And then, he who had set me apart from the day of my birth, and called me by his grace, saw fit to make his Son known to me, so that I could preach his gospel among the Gentiles. My first thought was not to hold any consultations with any human creature; I did not go up to Jerusalem to see those who had been apostles longer than myself; no, I went off into Arabia, and when I came back, it was to Damascus." (Galatians 1:15–17)

The journey to Rome was the adventure of a prisoner: arrest at Jerusalem, captivity at Caesarea, a two year detention at Rome awaiting a trial (which never took place). He was nearly sixty and his labors had worn him out, although they had never cast him down. At critical moments, the fighter awoke in him. Despite serious hopes of freedom, martyrdom was always on the horizon. His captivity was part of God's plan. As Paul had been called for the salvation of the Gentiles, working as an Apostle to bring them into the Church, he was now "a prisoner for Christ Jesus" on behalf of those same Gentiles (Ephesians 3:1). The sufferings he endured in his captivity were the completion of his work; after having been the minister of the Church by his apostolic labors, he completed in his apparent inaction the sufferings endured by Christ when he gave his body to death (Colossians 1:24–27).

What happened at Damascus was for Paul a revelation, "an apocalypse of the Son." It was, that is, an entry into the celestial world where the risen Christ reigns, but it was even more a confirmation by which Paul was appointed as prophet of the latter days: He was entrusted with divine authority to publish the mysteries he knew and to welcome men into the world of the spirit.

The glorified Christ whose Spirit had but lately flooded his being, planned to carry out through Paul his work of redemption and to pave the way for his final coming.[44]

Paul's messages in Thessalonians, Corinthians, Philippians, Galatians, Romans, Colossians, Ephesians, Titus and Timothy all depict Paul's faithfulness to Christ.

THE CLOSER WE WALK WITH GOD
THE CLEARER WE SEE HIS GUIDANCE.

The Lord's Grace to Paul

"I thank Christ Jesus our Lord, who has given me strength, that he considered me faithful, appointing me to his service. Even though I was once a blasphemer and a persecutor and a violent man, I was shown mercy because I acted in ignorance and unbelief. The grace of our Lord was poured out on me abundantly, along with the faith and love that are in Christ Jesus." (1Timothy 1:12–14)

Jesus Speaking About Paul

"This man is my chosen instrument to carry my name before the Gentiles and their kings and before the people of Israel. I will show him how much he must suffer for my name." (Acts 9:15-16)

---

[42] Excerpts taken from the book entitled, *The Spiritual Journey of St. Paul*, by Lucien Cerfaux. Copyright 1968, Sheed and Ward, New York, NY.

[43] Words have their destiny as books do. When the Christians of Jerusalem called their assembly by the term "church," who could have predicted its future? Of that future, Paul was the principal architect.

[44] Throughout this book I repeatedly mention that "God goes only where He is wanted." Evidently, an important exception is with Paul, and only God knows how many others.

After the Ascension

*"SOME THINGS ARE RIGHT,
SOME THINGS ARE WRONG,
ON THAT WE MUST AGREE,
BUT WHEN IT COMES TO TASTE AND STYLE,
THERE'S ROOM FOR LIBERTY."*[45]

---

[45] THE FOLLOWING "WRONGS" STATED ARE A PERSONAL ACCOUNT OF MY EXPERIENCES WITHIN THE CATHOLIC CHURCHES THAT I ATTENDED IN RHODE ISLAND.

M. Grace Ferri

SOME THINGS ARE RIGHT

What is RIGHT about the **Roman Catholic Church** (the most popular and wealthiest church in the world) is that it believes in the following: The Holy Bible is the whole truth. God is the Father Almighty, Creator of Heaven and Earth. Jesus Christ is His only Son, our Lord, who was conceived by the Holy Ghost, born of the Virgin Mary, suffered under Pontius Pilate, was crucified, died and was buried, and on the third day He arose from the dead. The Roman Catholic Church also believes in the resurrection of Jesus and His ascension into heaven where He now sits at the right hand of the Father, and that Jesus shall judge the living and the dead. They believe in the forgiveness of sins, stemming from the event of the cross of Jesus, and life everlasting (after physical death) and they embrace the mystery of the Holy Trinity.

The Catholic Church believes in confessing and repenting (although *not* exactly in the Biblical sense). It advocates strongly "Being Good and Doing Good Works," which is good advice. However, due to receiving the incomplete message of salvation, there are parishioners who think this is the way to be saved. The Catholic Church does believe in the angels and saints and the virtues leading to God. It also believes suffering and adversity are privileges when suffered for the sake of Jesus, who endured so much more suffering on the cross.

The yearly Catholic Charity Drive is extremely successful and in addition to the United States, the Church is greatly involved in Catholic teachings in Europe and other countries, furnishing substantial assistance in education to underdeveloped countries. The situation in missionary countries was affected by the fact that in many countries missionaries were more welcome as educators than as churchmen, and in some of these countries they were the first to institute general education.

The principle on which church education is conducted goes far beyond formal religious instructions. Children also learn the ways of worship, they are taught respect and reverence for prelates and clergy. Unfortunately, due to the shortage of nun teachers, many lay teachers have replaced them at the elementary school level. The same goes for priest teachers in the high schools. Studies were made in proving that the presence or absence of Roman Catholic schooling does not make a substantial difference in the religion of adults, except that more of those who had Roman Catholic schooling continued to attend Catholic Churches.

The First Holy Communion classes[46] and the Confirmation preparation classes are certainly better than no Christian instruction at all. **But upon completion, there are those who go no further in growing spiritually**. Then there are premarital sessions where couples go for counseling and instructions, not only regarding spiritual matters, but also advice on handling finances, etc. Hopefully, these preparation classes will be instrumental for better relationships within the marriage.

The conservatism of the Roman Catholic Church has always made it slow to accept new formulas which added something to the old. But development is *not* a process which has halted. Development, more frequently than not, arises from a factor outside the Roman Catholic Church.

The Church's greatest tribute to Catholicism is the Vatican City in Rome where the Pope (head of the Roman Catholic Church) presides. The Pope, as a rule, is well respected, loved and honored by many peoples of the world. He is the one visible symbol of the Roman Catholic Church and he is viewed as such both by believers and nonbelievers. He represents to believers a continuous chain originated with Jesus Christ, and to nonbelievers he represents a half billion people to whom he can speak with authority.

---

[46] I received my Christian beginnings through my First Communion classes instructed by the nuns at St. John's Church in Providence, RI. It was a foundation that I built on.

After the Ascension

SOME THINGS ARE WRONG

Christian faith and practice is *not* a matter of theological mental sharpness. In many cases, Catholic theologians have just as little a grasp of the meaning of their religion as anyone else. They know the story (facts) of Christ. They know the doctrines of the Trinity,[47] the incarnation, the virgin birth and the atonement, and can describe them with accuracy. But because there are those who may *not* comprehend what they mean, their description of them could be uninformative and lacking significance.

The Roman Catholic Mass is a presentation of the divine promise or testament of Christ. Too often, unfortunately, the sermons[48] leave something to be desired. In life, there are always exceptions to the rule, including the theologian situation and sermons offered. If clergy is *not* gifted in ways of preaching, this task should be given to someone else to "do it right." As a rule, words about salvation, how to be saved, or born again are omitted. Too many parishioners, unfortunately, think these phrases stem from an unchristian source even though they are mentioned in the gospels read from the altar.

"Salvation is by grace through faith."
(Ephesians 2:8–9)

Then there is the **annulment** situation. This was previously preached as an option only if the marriage was *not* consummated or if the marriage took place under false pretenses. (Example: if a spouse was already married or an escaped convict.) To date it is a different story. Annulments are given, usually for a **fee**, to those who want to remarry in the church without the stigma of divorce, as the church does *not* condone divorce. For many there are children involved. **Annulment, in reality, is just another glorified word for divorce.** It is a "play on words," which is ridiculous.

In regard to the **ceremony of baptism**, it was originally known to be a washing away of **original sin** that Adam and Eve were punished for in the Garden of Eden. The "christening" takes place in church with the **sprinkling** of water on the baby's forehead and with godparents present. But in recent years, the church is claiming that this ceremony is a born again experience, which is impossible for a baby to achieve. (Please refer to essay entitled *"Baptism"* for further details.)

Worshiping and praying to canonized saints[49] (as intercessors) was encouraged. JESUS IS OUR ONLY INTERCESSOR TO GOD. He alone can forgive us of our sins **after** confessing and repenting. Sins should be confessed and repented as soon as possible. Confession of sins should *not* be confined to once a week and "penance" (a Catholic expression) should be more than saying a few prayers. (Again, refer to essay entitled *"Repentance"*)

For some reason, in earlier years, Bible study classes were unheard of, maybe because they felt the parishioners were incapable of understanding the intricacies of the Bible. A person of holy discernment should do the teaching, and maybe this was a problem. Later, however, there were some Catholic Churches who did try to promote Bible study, but attendance was very limited. Hence, for the most part, this effort was dismissed.

At any given Mass, it has been observed that almost the

whole congregation receives the Holy Eucharist. Do the parishioners really realize the state of holiness that Jesus expects of them when they receive His Body? Only **after** a sincere confession and repentance (resulting in a pure and holy soul/heart) should "communion" be taken. Unfortunately, many are probably still harboring sins that are *not* dealt with, but still receive the Holy Eucharist. Going to Mass and receiving His Body are *not* guarantees of being destined for the Kingdom of Heaven. It is in the same category as being "good" and doing "good works." Only **after** having a personal relationship with Jesus are good works considered by the Lord.[50] Holiness should exist in our everyday life, *not* just on the Sabbath. Attending Mass does not excuse us from "right" living after church services. **IF JUST BEING "GOOD" GOT US TO HEAVEN, THEN GOD MADE A BIG MISTAKE BY LETTING HIS SON SUFFER IMMENSELY FOR OUR SINS.**

After all is said and done, it's better to be a Catholic Christian than to be an atheist, belong to an unholy cult, or worship idols and graven images. Of course, we know that the Lord's desire is for all of us to become Born Again Christians.

THE TRUTH WILL SET YOU FREE,
BUT FIRST IT *MAY* MAKE YOU MISERABLE.

"These people honor me with their lips, but their hearts are far from me. They worship me in vain. Their teachings are but rules taught by men."
(Matthew 15:8–9)

> "... *outwardly (you) appear righteous to men, but inside you are hypocrisy and lawlessness.*"
> *(Matthew 23:28)*

---

[47] The Trinity is the unity of Father, Son and Holy Spirit as three persons in one Godhead according to **Christian** dogma. This belief comes, without doubt, by Faith and Trust in God.

[48] I have attended Catholic Masses for many years and have never heard a sermon with reference to becoming "Born Again" or "Saved." I am hoping the Catholic Church will one day realize the error of its ways and become a complete Christian Church according to the Bible.

[49] The Catholic rosary beads are used quite frequently as a powerful tool for praying to the Blessed Mother. However, this depicts putting the Blessed Mother before her Son, Jesus, which is biblically incorrect. It would be more meaningful to Jesus for the rosary beads to be **ten** "Our Fathers" and **one** "Hail Mary" per decade. Our Blessed Mother would want it this way.

[50] I am sure that to many I must sound like a finger-wagging moralist imposing rules of conduct on the church. I am just a messenger of what is in my heart and of what I have witnessed in the Catholic Church for the past seventy years.

After the Ascension

TASTE AND STYLE

As a rule, *"Anything done in good faith should not be criticized."* However, there are always exceptions to the rule.

For instance: The garb, candles, Holy water, incense, kissing of rings, kneeling and the sign of the Cross are of good faith. However, rosary beads, novenas, spiritual bouquets and patron saints are *not* biblically correct.[51]

The following italicized excerpts were taken from *The Roman Catholic Church* by John L. McKenzie.

Papacy. *The Papacy is the most obvious and distinctive feature of Roman Catholicism. The powers of the* **Pope** *are defined in Cannon Law in words taken from the First Vatican Council as "The supreme and full power of jurisdiction over the universal church both in matters of faith and morals and in matters of discipline and government." The Pope has authority over each and every Catholic church as well as over each and every Catholic pastor and believer, and is independent of any human authority.*

College of Cardinals. *They are the most powerful "group" within the church. The college has two classes. One class includes cardinals who are residential bishops and who remain in the jurisdiction which they govern. Cardinals who are not residential bishops are to live in Rome and to take posts in the papal administration. Cardinals are appointed personally by the Pope.*

Bishops. *Each bishop is supreme in his diocese having no superior other than the Roman Pontiff. The Bishops alone possess jurisdictional power in their diocese and are captains of major intensive business enterprises.*

Monsignors. Many who are not Catholic heads find the institution of Monsignors puzzling. This is purely a title of honor granted to priests and conveys no office or jurisdiction. Monsignor, my lord, is an Anglicized form of the Italian style of polite address. Priests who are called "Monsignor" are honorary members of the papal household. Some are called "Right Reverend" and hold the title permanently. Others with the lesser title "Very Reverend," their honor expires at the death of the Pope. The Monsignor is entitled to wear a purple gown or a gown with purple trimmings. The honor is obtained for his priests by the Bishop. It generally attests either a high ranking post in the Episcopal chancery or long and distinguished service in the pastoral ministry.

Pastors. The Pastor is chosen by the Bishop and is not only the head of the parish, but also the head of the household. Details of housekeeping, such as the cuisine, the furniture and the use of heat and electricity, etc., is his responsibility. The built-in difficulties of the life of the rectory are enough to assure one that the humanity of both pastors and **assistants** must be remarkable to make it succeed as well as it does.

In addition to the church, the buildings often include the rectory, school, residence for the religious who teach in the school and possibly a hall for meetings whereby the pastor is the responsible administrator of the parish property under the bishop.

Priests. The priest is taught that when the "Catholic" experiences the church, he should experience Jesus Christ. It is the priest's responsibility to see that the experience is authentic. Where this conviction is deep and genuine it gives the priest a personal power which can be neither described nor measured. His *power should rest simply on authentic, transparent and personal holiness. His sacred power is communicated by ordination. The development of priesthood came when the single "church" community became too numerous for the single bishop to serve. His sacred power consists of the power to preach, to administer the sacraments and to govern.*

Nuns. *Nuns take their vows at a ceremony similar to a wedding ceremony of Christians whereby becoming married to Jesus. Nuns are at the bottom of the list, salary-wise. They run hospitals, orphanages, schools. Some also do various household chores, along with duties like gardening, etc. In earlier years some even took on the heavier tasks like firing up the boilers in the morning.* As teachers, they leave a strong impact on the children they teach. They have contributed greatly toward the Catholic well-being.

Today, like the priests, there is a shortage of nuns and many lay people have replaced them in the schools, hospitals, orphanages, and otherwise.

In today's times, many aspects of being a nun has changed. They have more privileges and the dress code is more lenient. The heavier chores are now most likely given to other hired people. As a rule, the nuns are exceptionally dedicated to God.

Laity. *In Roman Catholicism the Laity are passive members of the church. The laity is the governed, the recipients of the sacraments and the listeners. Of course, the laity is not simply inactive, but the long tradition of church office and functions leaves no place in the structure for lay activity. The one activity which is steadily and seriously urged on the laity is the activity of supporting the economic structure of the Roman Catholic Church.*

There are many more aspects connected to the Catholic religion, like the sacraments, extreme unction, Ecumenical Council, exorcists, lectors, altar boys (and now girls). Most importantly to Catholicism is the celebration of the Mass and the Holy Eucharist, where they duplicate the powerful presentation by Jesus of the Last Supper, whereby dispensing to parishioners the wafer depicting the Body of Christ. The wine, however, which represents the Blood of Christ, is taken only by the priest. They perform this sacred ritual at every Mass and feel that this and the dispensing of the Holy Eucharist to the congregation is the epitome of Catholicism in the ways of saving souls for Heaven. And they would be correct if the whole ritual was understood **properly** by the parishioners.

In itself, going to Mass weekly (even daily) and receiving the Holy Eucharist does not make one a candidate for the Kingdom of Heaven. But, unfortunately, an ample percentage of the parishioners who receive the so-called Blessed Sacrament of Communion could be ignorant of the holy Christian aspects involved before "receiving." Jesus will not enter muddled and insincere souls. But as mentioned before, too many Catholics have not been preached to regarding the Biblical rendition of "Being Saved." Hence, too many are ignorant in this detailed matter and think that because they attend Mass and receive the Body of Christ they are recipients of God's favorable love and eventually the Kingdom of Heaven.

According to Catholic teachings, starting with First Communion classes, upon receiving the Body and Blood of Christ, Catholics should be completely cleansed of all their sins **after** confessing and repenting (with the understanding that the person would strive never to sin again) whereby, any sins would be forgiven over and over again by confessing to a priest. **God wants us to confess to Jesus and repent almost immediately, not once a week as the Catholic religion advocates.** The confessional teachings are efficient for youngsters through their First Communion classes.[52]

It is amazing how almost the entire congregation arises to receive the Holy Eucharist. Could it be possible that these parishioners have sincerely confessed and repented? (Refer to essay entitled "An Explanation of Repentance.") And most importantly, does **everyone** who accepts the Body and Blood of Christ truly understand the importance of Jesus being "Number One" in their life and how they should continuously strive to follow His Father's will? **God's "will" is more than following the Ten Commandments and some church laws.** If, by some miracle, these are the holy conditions that exist in all parishioners who partake in "receiving," then the Catholic Church is correct in believing that this is a true act for salvation. (For further clarification, refer to essay entitled, "Transform Your Heart.")

> BEING INCLUDED IN GOD'S FAMILY
> IS THE HIGHEST HONOR AND
> THE GREATEST PRIVILEGE
> YOU WILL EVER RECEIVE.

"While they were eating, Jesus took bread, gave thanks and broke it, and gave it to his disciples saying, 'Take it, this is my body.' Then he took the cup, gave thanks and offered it to them, and

they all drank from it. 'This is my blood of the covenant which is poured out for many,' He said to them." (Mark 14:22–24)

---

[51] Excerpts taken from the book entitled *The Roman Catholic Church* by John L. McKenzie. Copyright 1969, Holt, Rinehart and Winston, Houston, TX.

[52] I thank God for my very good childhood beginnings through my First Communion classes instructed by the devoted nuns at St. John's Catholic Church in Providence, RI. However, as an adult I grew spiritually due to watching the Protestant Christian preachers on television.

After the Ascension

PRIESTHOOD

(Catholic)

The following italicized passage is taken from *The Roman Catholic Church* by John L. McKenzie.

Mandated celibacy has become an issue, in part, because of the declining numbers of vocations to the priesthood, seemingly related to the celibacy requirements. Many young men see the priesthood as something they might consider, but they are unwilling to commit themselves to a celibate lifetime.[53]

Jesus' words, "You are Peter and upon this rock I will build my church" (Matthew 16:18), conferred upon Peter the primary authority for leading Jesus' followers. Jesus did not seem to be bothered by Peter's commitment to his wife and family when He called upon Peter to follow Him or gave Peter the role of being the "Rock" on which he would build Jesus' church. Peter, as a married man, ministered to his community in Apostolic times. As a married man, he led the first church council at Jerusalem. Peter left quite an example of leadership and dedication for the faithful to follow. Even though Peter had denied Jesus three times to save his own skin, Jesus still chose him to be the leader of His following. This idea that Peter was one of us, a real person who was married, had family, exhibited weakness, makes it clear that in Biblical times celibacy was not a requirement.

Today, however, celibacy renounces all physical sexual relationships and is a requirement for those responding to the call to serve as Catholic priests. It has become another one of those debatable issues for Catholics. The development of priesthood came when the single "church" community became too numerous for the single bishop to serve. The sacred power consists of the power to preach, administer the sacraments and to govern. Sacred power is communicated by ordination.

It is unfortunate for Catholic parishioners that so many priests are lacking in the gift of eloquent speech, whereby depriving the parishioners the chance to understand and grow in the ways of God. Too many Catholics remain what is called "Baby Christians," remembering, for the most part, what they were taught at First Communion and Confirmation preparation classes. Since many are unable to understand the "Bible," they count on what is preached to them by the priests at the Catholic Masses.

Unless priests can see the sermon as an opportunity and a challenge, a personal encounter between the people and themselves in which the reality of the church lives, they will not have the spark which even a routine good sermon demands. It is hardly necessary to add that good preaching means that the priest is what he utters and this is more than the "good example." The priest can communicate only the faith which he has. **One can say that renewal and reform with Roman Catholicism will march as far and as fast as good preaching will take it.**[54]

> *"If ye continue in my word, then are ye my disciples indeed." (John 8:31)*

---

[53] Excerpts taken from the book entitled *The Roman Catholic Church* by John L. McKenzie. Copyright 1969, Holt, Rinehart and Winston, Houston, TX.

[54] We need to be loving and supporting of one another's Christian ministry. We should restore the ones who fail, not reject and condemn.

After the Ascension

FROM TRADITION TO TRUTH

(His Struggle With Being A Catholic Priest)

The following is the testimony of Richard Benett, a **former** Catholic priest:[55] from *The Good News in RI*.

By the time I was about five or six years of age, Jesus Christ was a very real person to me, but so also were Mary and the saints. I can identify easily with others in traditional Catholic nations in Europe and with Hispanics and Filipinos who put Jesus, Mary, Joseph and other saints all in one boiling pot of faith.

Not having any idea of the true salvation message, I decided that I truly did have call to be a missionary. This idea of gaining salvation through suffering and prayer is also the basic message of Fatima and Lourdes, and I sought to win my own salvation as well as the salvation of others by such suffering and prayer.

I had a freak accident, splitting the back of my head and hurting my spine in many places. Without thus coming close to death I doubt that I would ever have gotten out of my self-satisfied state. Prayer showed its emptiness as I cried out to God in my pain. In the suffering that I went through in the weeks after the accident, I began to find some comfort in direct personal prayer (the Roman Catholic Church's official prayer for clergy) and the Rosary and began to pray using parts of the Bible itself. This was a very slow process. I did not know my way through the Bible and the little I had learned over the years had taught me more to distrust it rather than to trust it. My training in philosophy and in the theology of Thomas Aquinas left me helpless, so that coming into the Bible now to find the Lord was like going into a huge dark woods without a map. I continued my personal search into the Bible, but it did not much affect the work we were doing; rather it showed me how little I really knew about the Lord and His Word. It was at this time that Philippians 3:10 became the cry of my heart, "That I may know him, and the power of his resurrection . . ."

It began to dawn on me that in Biblical terms, the Bishops I knew in the Catholic Church were not Biblical believers.

They were for the most part pious men taken up with devotion to Mary and the Rosary and loyal to Rome, but not one had any idea of the finished work of salvation, that Christ's work is done, that salvation is personal and complete. They all preached penance for sin, human suffering, religious deeds, "the way of man" rather than the Gospel of grace. But by God's grace I saw that it was not through the Roman Church nor by any kind of works that one is saved, "For by the grace are ye saved through faith; and that not of yourselves: it is the gift of God: Not the works, lest any man should boast" (Ephesians 2:8–9).

I left the Roman Catholic Church when I saw that life in Jesus Christ was not possible while remaining true to Roman Catholic doctrine. I was amazed at how easy it is for the Lord's grace to be effective when only the Bible is used to present Jesus Christ. This contrasted with the cobwebs of church tradition that had so clouded my 21 years in missionary garments in Trinidad, 21 years without the real message.

To explain the abundant life of which Jesus spoke and which I now enjoy, no better words could be used than those of Romans 8:1–2: "There is therefore now no condemnation to them which are in Christ Jesus, who walk not after the flesh, but after the Spirit. For the law of the Spirit of life in Christ Jesus hath made me free from the law of sin and death." It is not just that I have been freed from the Roman Catholic system, but that I have become a new creature in Christ. It is by the grace of God, and nothing but His grace, that I have gone from dead works into new life.

God gives us the faith to be born again, making it possible for us to acknowledge Christ as our substitute. It was Christ who paid the price for our sins: sinless, yet He was crucified. This is the true Gospel message. Is faith enough? Yes, born-again faith is enough. That faith, born of God, will result in good works including repentance: "For we are his workmanship, created in Christ Jesus unto good works, which God had before ordained that we should walk in them" (Ephesians 2:10).

In repenting, we put aside, through God's strength, our

former way of life and our former sins. It does not mean that we cannot sin again, but it does mean that our position before God has changed. We are called children of God, for so indeed we are. If we do sin, it is a relationship problem with the Father which can be resolved, not a problem of losing our position as a child of God in Christ, for this position is irrevocable. In Hebrews 10:10, the Bible says it so wonderfully: "... we are sanctified through the offering of the body of Jesus Christ once for all."

The finished work of Christ Jesus on the Cross is sufficient and complete. As you trust solely in this finished work, a new life which is born of the Spirit will be yours—you will be born again.

Richard Bennett is a native of Ireland. He returned there in 1996 on an evangelistic tour. He now lives in Portland, Oregon U.S.A. He teaches a workshop at Multnomah Bible College on "Catholicism in the Light of Biblical Truth." His greatest joy is door-to-door witnessing. He has produced three series of radio broadcasts. A fourth series is about to begin in the Philippines on DWTI and DVRO radio stations. He is co-editor of his book and founder of the ministry named "Berean Beacon."

---

[55]Excerpts taken from *The Good News in RI*, Vol. 2 No. 12, December 2003.

M. GRACE FERRI

THE BRAIN

(Good Health Tips)

The following italicized portion is from the magazine *Prevention.*

*The mind is unlimited in its capacity to learn. Scientists say the average person uses as little as ten percent of the brain; the rest of the brain is available but untapped. Scientific research has also shown the brain has two sides (or hemispheres) and they function very differently. Most classroom teachings only make use of the "left" hemisphere. The "left" hemisphere works with facts and logical point by point thinking. But the "right" hemisphere works with **feeling, fantasy, imagination, mental imagery and intuition**—and when both hemispheres of the brain are involved in learning, a professor of psychology states: "Learning is easier, faster and much more fun. Mental imagery ('right' brain thinking) sparks the powerful subconscious mind into action."*[56]

*For many, there were times in our lives we were told that daydreaming and fantasy may not be good for us. People are taught to think only in words—to hear words in their head. However, we learn much more effectively if we make a **picture** in our head about the material we are dealing with. Advice to students is to "Picture yourself in the book. Feel that it's happening to you. Make up a story about the material and 'see' it. Get the right half of the brain involved." The professors believe that mental imagery isn't only for book-learning; it helps you achieve any skill. For instance, make a picture in your head of getting along with your mate, communicating successfully with your boss or winning at a sport. If you don't make pictures in your head, you may not be tapping into your "right" hemisphere.*

Fear and anxiety can block the learning process. There is a fear that comes from remembering a previous painful and difficult learning experience. Many times a young person's learning ability is often criticized and belittled, but that criticism has nothing to do with his real learning ability. In older people there is the fear of failure and the fear that the mind can't remember as well as it used to.

*A **relaxation skill** is the most crucial element to improve learning ability. "Yoga" or "Transcendental Meditation"*[57] *are somewhat helpful in calming the mind and making a person more receptive to what he has to learn.* **Praying to the Lord is the ultimate skill for relaxation. And being obedient to the Lord will bring us great joy and contentment.**

*Then there's **music** while studying. It's believed any **soothing music** will do. A professor at the University of Toronto was one of the first people to conduct studies on music and learning. Soothing music not only makes a wonderful background for studying, but also when indulging in creative activities.*

It is a well known fact that improper eating and drinking habits can hinder our bodies both physically and mentally. However, many feel that eating and drinking in a healthy, sensible manner should result in maintaining a healthy body. But what we're finding true today is that even good eating and drinking habits could result in vitamin and nutrient deficiencies, not only due to the way food is processed today, but also due to the intake of drugs (including those prescribed) and excessive alcohol. For instance, **one** example is that the excessive consumption of alcohol depletes Vitamin B-1, affecting the process of healing in our bodies. **Beware—it is possible to overdose on certain vitamins.** Our first priority is for us to "correct" what can be corrected by eliminating bad habits. Then we should look into taking proper vitamin and nutrient supplements according to our individual needs.

The brain isn't nourished only by food and drink. If a person sits in a cramped position in a windowless room with no fresh air, he's not going to be able to concentrate or memorize "well" because his brain isn't getting enough oxygen. Deep breathing techniques improve learning ability and oxygenation of the blood.

Therefore, your life ability will improve with **mental imagery, relaxation, restful music, good diet, sensible exercise, proper sunlight, massage therapy, deep breathing techniques, sufficient water and sleep, proper vitamin supplements and praying.**[58] Also, we should make an effort to learn more in ways of betterment concerning our jobs and our relationships. Of course, the ultimate relationship is with Jesus, our Lord and Savior. Our relationship with Him, our self and other people are all connected—they all affect each other. Our sense of self-worth and self-esteem comes from an understanding of God and His love for us.

LAUGHTER IS THE BEST MEDICINE; IT CAN BE BENEFICIAL TO INTERNAL HEALINGS.

> *"Understanding is a fountain of life to those who have it, but folly brings punishment to fools." (Proverbs 16:22)*
>
> *"A merry heart does good, like medicine, But a broken spirit dries the bone." (Proverbs 17:22)*

---

[56] Excerpts taken from the magazine *Prevention,* November, 1980, Volume 32, Number 11. Copyright Rodale Press, Inc., Emmaus, PA.

[57] Before I gave my life to Jesus, I used the technique of Transcendental Meditation in trying to achieve "peace of mind." It helped somewhat, but the satisfying achievement came when I "gave up" my Mantra and called on the Name of Jesus.

[58] Extreme stress could cause both external and internal problems in our body. Exercising the options mentioned in this essay could alleviate many serious ailments.

After the Ascension

WITH GOD ALL THINGS ARE POSSIBLE

(Matthew 19:26)

*I realize fully that the following two theories will either be considered **food for thought or just plain garbage**. I have never read or heard anything regarding these issues in relation to my summaries. They stem from my personal "brainstorming" and "imagination," and they are just hypotheses.*[59] *I hope the Lord is not too upset with my deductions. I fully realize He alone is in control of everything and that we were made by God and for God and life will never make sense unless this is understood.*

> *"I know a man in Christ who fourteen years ago was caught up to the **third heaven**. Whether it was in the body or out of the body I do not know—God knows. And I know that this man—whether in the body or apart from the body I do not know, but God knows—was caught up to paradise." (2 Corinthians 12:2–4)*

---

[59]**Like Paul, in 2 Corinthians 12:2–4, I do not know—God knows.** I know some things for sure (according to the Bible), but with reference to non-biblical deductions, only God knows whether my theories are "food for thought" or "just plain garbage."

M. Grace Ferri

BIRTH OF A THEORY

Three Heavens

(A Taste of Uncertainty)

It all came about when I started to think deeply, years ago, and asked myself the question, "If only the Born Again Christians go to Heaven and the evil go to hell, where do the basically good people go who are *not* good enough for Heaven and *not* evil enough for hell?[60] And then I came across *"Third Heaven"* mentioned briefly in the Bible (2 Corinthians 12:2). Another source came from a well-known preacher on television. At the very end of his Sunday program, he stated, *"Some people believe there are Seven Heavens, but I personally believe there are only three."* It was then that I began to "brainstorm" about the *"Three Heavens."* I asked a few knowledgeable Christians if they knew anything about this subject and nobody came up with any explanations.[61]

It has been definitely established that only the souls of the **Born Again Christians** enter the Kingdom of Heaven and the souls of the evil (who remain evil until their last breath) will definitely go to Hell. **So, again, where do all the other souls go who are *not* quite good enough for Heaven and are *not* evil enough for Hell???**

For example, there's the "lukewarm Christians" who tether back and forth between God and Satan, making up their own rules about Christianity. They claim to be Christians, but are portraying a different kind of Christ, ***never* striving to become complete Christians and remain in their comfort zone.** Hence, there has to be a level in the Heavens for these tainted souls who are *not* evil enough for the fires of hell. Surprisingly, so-called

Purgatory came to mind, **but *NOT* exactly the way the Catholics portray it.**

I realize "Purgatory"[62] is *not* mentioned in the Bible, but neither is the word "Trinity." Purgatory is in the Catholic index and is briefly alluded to in the Catholic Bible. **However, all forms of prayers from loved ones left behind will *NOT* help to elevate souls from Purgatory to the Kingdom of Heaven. Only God has the power to do this.** And the transition of the lukewarm Christians most likely takes place **after** the punishment (suffering) has been completed in full and the soul is thoroughly cleansed and purified and made fit for the Kingdom of Heaven. Then there are those "good people" who worship only God the Father, and others who may strive to be good, but, unfortunately, worship other images or none at all.

Again, there has to be a level in the Heavens for these very tainted souls who are basically good, but *not* evil enough for the fires of hell. Since God is *"just," "fair"* and *"righteous,"* He will deal with every person on the basis of the "light" received, the opportunities granted, the extent of one's wickedness and the motive behind the deeds. ***However, only Jesus is in control of the destiny of our souls and eventually our mystical bodies.***

*"In the beginning God created the **heavens**."*
(Genesis 1:1)

---

[60]This essay was formulated in the year 1993.

[61]The Protestant Christians believe there is only Heaven and hell. However, the Catholic Christians believe there is Heaven, purgatory and hell. In ways of belief, there are always exceptions to the rule.

[62]The dictionary defines Purgatory as a place or state of temporary suffering or misery. Also, an intermediate state after death for expiatory purification; a place or state of punishment. *According to Roman Catholic doctrine, the souls of those who died in God's grace may make satisfaction of past sins and so become fit for Heaven.

*The Roman Catholic doctrine, regarding the souls who died in God's Grace, is biblically incorrect. **The souls of those who died in God's Grace are definitely saved** and after the first judgment by Jesus these souls/spirits will abide in the Kingdom of Heaven without any punishment.

M. GRACE FERRI

SUMMARY OF THREE HEAVENS

(A Hypothesis)

HOT (On Fire For The Lord)

Third Heaven: (Highest Level)

Could very well be for the souls of those who died in God's grace. The realm in which God's "will" was fulfilled. Where Christ reigns and where only the souls of the Born Again Christians preside until the time when Christ unites bodies with souls and brings these saints down, along with His angels, to a new earth. These people, when alive "in Christ," heard the call of God and rushed to meet His needs. They were obedient to God for they knew it brought honor and glory to Him by making His Son Jesus the center of their life. Also their gifts from the Holy Spirit were honored and exercised.

LUKEWARM (Fell Short of Being Born Again)

Second Heaven: (Middle Level)

*Could be an intermediate state after death for expiatory purification. A place or state of punishment **by God**. No amount of prayers from loved ones left behind can elevate these souls to the Kingdom of Heaven. Prayers and flowers should be for the "living." Possibly, **after** the suffering (which is allotted to them by God according to their sins), these souls are fully cleansed, purified and **made fit for the Kingdom of Heaven**. While alive on earth, these people did not fully honor Jesus and were often disobedient to His Father's "will" up until their last breath. God could not have been fully pleased with their thoughts and* actions; therefore, upon death, their souls most likely were deprived from the Kingdom of Heaven at the first immediate judgment by Jesus. Hopefully, these souls who were not good enough for the Kingdom of Heaven and not evil enough for hell could possibly be given a second chance by God to experience "Everlasting Life."

(Called purgatory by Catholics, but their perception is quite different than above)

COLD (Two Groups)

First Heaven: (Lowest Level)

A. Is probably for those "poor" souls who were never made aware of the Almighty God, His Son Jesus, or the Holy Spirit, never having been exposed to the existence of God or the truths of the Bible. And up until their last breath they remained ignorant to the joys of being saved. God is fairest of all, hence, in His infinite wisdom, the punishment meted out in that "day" will probably be moderate indeed for that poor benighted heathen who never heard the gospel in contrast to the terrible fate of those who **knew** the way of salvation, but deliberately refused it. The punishment for the heathen could very well be that they will forever be separated from Jesus without ever experiencing "Life Everlasting" with Jesus in the Kingdom of Heaven.

B. Included in this level could possibly be the souls of those who loved God but rejected Jesus as His Son due to their religious upbringing, and also for the souls of those who were basically good, but knew not the things of God due to inborn feelings of indifference to spiritual ways and were strictly for the

world. *After God's punishment, this group will forever be separated from Jesus (like the heathen).*
Jesus Speaking

> *"I know your deeds, that you are neither cold nor hot. I wish that you were either one or the other. So because you are lukewarm—neither hot nor cold—I am about to spit you out of my mouth."* **(Revelations 3:15–16)**

HELL:

*Of course, hell is for the souls of the **forever** wicked, the God haters, the bitter ones who were the devil's advocates, who caused misery and unhappiness. Usually, Satan was their god. Many were "wolves in sheep's clothing."* **Their complete dishonor to the Holy Spirit will cause them everlasting pain.**

> *"And so I tell you, every sin and blasphemy against the Spirit will NOT be forgiven. Anyone who speaks a word against the Son of Man, will be forgiven, but anyone who speaks against the Holy Spirit will NOT be forgiven either in this age or the age to come." (Matthew 12:31–32)*

As mentioned before—all I know for sure is that the souls of the Born Again Christians (the true believers) go to the Kingdom of Heaven and the souls of the evil go to hell. **There are two kinds of evil;** the ones who know right from wrong and somewhere along the way were shown the "light," but performed evil acts anyway, **never** confessing or repenting. Hell is their inheritance.

And then there are those (probably in Hitler's category) who exist with no knowledge of God and are completely ignorant of the ways of the Lord. They know what is "right" for themselves and unwarily perform evil acts against the Word of God. They are lacking in compassion and think they are "right" even when they are completely wrong. Ironically, God is so merciful that he probably will grant the **latter** evil ones some kind of understanding. Since Jesus knows our hearts, He alone will discern on the first judgment which transpires immediately after death.

What happens to the souls of the GOOD, who were *not* good enough for Heaven and *not* "evil" enough for hell, still remains a mystery!! My theories stem from a brainstorming, imaginative and explorative mind. **I realize fully that only God knows what is in store for us in the full truth of the hereafter.**[63]

DECIDE WHAT GOD WOULD DECIDE.
YOU CAN NEVER MAKE A WRONG CHOICE AND GET A RIGHT RESULT.

"I will punish the world for its evil, the wicked for their sins. I will put an end to the arrogance of the haughty and will humble the pride of the ruthless." (Isaiah 13:11)

"Imagination is more important than knowledge." (Albert Einstein)

---

[63] I meditated for years regarding my essay on "Birth Of A Theory." Much later I was exposed to the reincarnation theory, hence a revamped essay was formulated not only for those who are "toying" with the idea of reincarnation, but also for those who truly believe it.

M. Grace Ferri

REBIRTH OF A THEORY
(Reincarnation)

TRUE OR FALSE? The theory of "reincarnation" has to be confronted as it is a popular and highly debatable issue. Reincarnation is an ill-founded belief held uncritically by an interested group. This essay was formulated not only for those **toying** with the idea of "Reincarnation," but also for those who firmly believe in this theory.[64] Long after writing the Three Heavens essay, I heard a couple of statements that "boggled" my mind. One from a movie on television where the young lady at the very end of the movie (which was *not* at all related to spirituality) commented, *"Maybe we will have a second chance to come back and 'do it right.'"* (No further comments by her).

Then I heard a statement made by a person on the radio and at the very end of his presentation he stated something very similar, *"Maybe we are born again with a brand new soul in order to 'get it right.'"* This last statement had nothing to do with what he was previously commenting about.

Of course, with my state of mind, I began "brainstorming" **all over again** about the theory of the Three Heavens and prayed to the Holy Spirit to give me guidance in this new deduction.

> *"See to it that no one captivate you with an empty, seductive philosophy." (Colossians 2:8)*

So, are the previous statements heard on television and radio **just seductive philosophies**? Formerly, I dismissed the reincarnation theory as being completely **un**christian-like and senseless, especially when people talked about coming back as creatures of all sorts. However, like the words "Trinity" and "Purgatory"—"Reincarnation" is *not* mentioned in the Bible. It is a known fact that there are multitudes of people who are "toying" with the idea of reincarnation and the possibility of coming back as animals, birds and other creatures. And there are those who feel that they have already come back as a prominent person from the past (Marie Antoinette seems to be a favorite by many). **I know for a fact that thoughts regarding reincarnation are harbored in both non-Christians and Christians alike,** but, evidently, for the most part, *not* in a clear, sensible fashion. Could it be possible that the "Born Again" phrase used in the Bible constitutes their beliefs?

I'M ASSUMING AT THIS POINT THAT MANY ARE THOROUGHLY DISGUSTED WITH THESE WRITINGS. I was formerly appalled by the idea of reincarnation. The previous statements made on television and radio opened up my mind to a new way of thinking. **I am still very doubtful as to the validity of this hypothesis. However, since God can do anything, anything is possible**.

After extensive brainstorming, deep meditation and prayers to the Holy Spirit to guide me regarding my hypothesis, my choice for the souls in the **lowest level of the Heavens**, who rejected Jesus altogether, could possibly be completely cleansed and purified by God, like the souls of the lukewarm Christians. (Refer to essay entitled, "Summary of Three Heavens). Hence, these souls who rejected Christ could also be "made fit" for **unborn** babies so that the formerly **un**christian soul could be given another chance to "get it right" IN A BRAND NEW BODY. **It seems evident that the brand new soul would definitely have to be planted by God at the moment of human conception.**

So, what does "get it right" mean? It means to become a Born Again Christian, for according to Jesus, when speaking to Nicodemus, *"Only if you are born again can you see the Kingdom of God."* (John 3:3) I somehow feel if the new soul does *not* "get it right" on God's first effort of reincarnation that it could be in God's plan for the same soul to be replanted over and over again until the person does "get it right."[65]

I was very skeptical about including this essay in my book. I realize that I will be subject to controversy as reincarnation is an UNHOLY summarization for most Christians. But, realistically, what is so wrong about the REBIRTH (after God's fair punishment) of a perfectly cleansed and purified soul implanted by God in a brand new body to "get it right?" Also, there are probably multitudes of people walking around with these kinds of souls in hopes of God wanting these people to strive to reach the ultimate, which is to become Born Again and ultimately be with Jesus in Paradise.

Could it be that the real reason why certain authoritative Christians (past and present) have *not* elaborated on the reincarnation theory is simply because there would be too many Christians who would *not* "strive" to be Born Again Christians if it became known that they could have a second chance (maybe even more than one chance) to "do it right?" Unfortunately, there could be many who would take their chances by *not* conforming to God's wish for "all to be saved." HENCE, THE FOOLISH ONES WOULD GIVE THEIR SOULS, IN PART, TO THE DEVIL IF THEY WERE UNDER THE ILLUSION THAT THEIR SOULS COULD BE REINCARNATED AND WHEREBY SOMEONE ELSE COULD "WORK" AT BECOMING BORN AGAIN, **EVIDENTLY TAKING THEIR CHANCES WITH THE DEPTH OF GOD'S PUNISHMENT**. This deduction is certainly a VALID reason for wanting to keep this reincarnation theory under control. *No one knows about that day or hour, not even the angels in Heaven, nor the Son, but only the Father. As it was in the days of Noah, so it will be at the coming of the Son of Man"* (Matthew 24:36–37).

BUT there is a *"Catch-22"*[66] condition and that is that **no one knows but the Father Himself** when Jesus will come again to raise firstly the "dead in Christ" and then secondly the "living in Christ." Upon this second coming of Jesus, this is when all those who are *not* "Born Again" will remain on earth to face the horrible conditions of the Tribulation period (refer to essay entitled *"The Tribulation Period"*). However, the Jewish people, for the most part, believe it will be His First Coming. Of course, the true Christian believers know it will be His Second Coming.

Who am I to think these writings could possibly be valid? But this is what my imagination has given to me. Maybe it is wrong, maybe it is partially right. I know the Kingdom of Heaven is "right" and I know hell is "right." However, this is the insight I received into the mystery of the hereafter. **I fully realize only God knows our true fate.**

These deductions are strictly personal. I have *never* heard or read anything pertaining to the spiritual order of the three levels or my very questionable theory of reincarnation. Maybe it has already been said or written. I PRAY TO THE LORD THAT MY IMAGINATIVE AND EXPLORATIVE MIND WILL *NOT* HINDER MY CHANCES OF BEING WITH HIM IN THE HEREAFTER.

If you are truly concerned about the hereafter, then start turning your life completely around IMMEDIATELY and do "what is right" to be with Jesus one day in the Kingdom of Heaven. DO NOT DEPEND ON BEING REINCARNATED AS IT COULD VERY WELL BE NOTHING BUT A FARCE.[67]

> *IMAGINATION IS MORE IMPORTANT THAN KNOWLEDGE (Albert Einstein)*

> *"... I tell you, **now** is the time of God's favor, **now** is the day of salvation." (2 Corinthians 6:2)*

> *"More powerful than the roar of many waters, more powerful than the breakers of the sea, **powerful in the heavens** is the Lord." (Psalms 93:4)*

---

[64] This essay was formulated in the year 2000.

[65] And then there is deja vu where there are those who feel they have experienced a situation that is very familiar to them, but they really don't remember the incident ever occurring in their present life. It happened to me in Pompeii on our visit to Italy in 1980. At the time, I really didn't understand my feelings as I was totally against things of this nature.

[66] With reference to the phrase "Catch-22," it is a frustrating situation in which one is trapped by constrictive regulations or conditions.

[67] I am praying that the Lord will forgive me if I am "off-base" regarding my theories, as they were written in good faith. He has given us a free will, for the most part, to **choose** our fate in the "hereafter." All I know is that Jesus is totally in me on earth and I truly want to be with Him in Paradise one day.

After the Ascension

FAVORITE QUOTES

"Forgiveness is the greatest power the world will ever know."

"Born Again Christians are not perfect—they just try harder and forgive more readily."

"When your opinion is ridiculed, a true sign of greatness is silence—silence with a Holy indifference."

"Common sense is not Divine sense."

"It is better to have loved and lost than never to have loved at all."

*"Anything done in good faith should not be criticized."

"Some people don't get mad—they get even."

"Actions speak louder than words."

"A feeling is neither right nor wrong. It is the action that counts. However, we should pray for negative feelings to be short-lived. Harboring these feelings can become harmful."

*"There is a difference between complaining and explaining."

"You have not converted a man because you have silenced him."

"How would we know the magnitude of our own worth without someone worthless attacking it?"

"No act of kindness, no matter how small, is ever wasted."

*"There will always be exceptions to the rule. Also, there are times we should 'bend' due to certain circumstances."

"We should hate what God hates and we should love what God loves."

"There are people who are often in an unaware, incompetent bracket. Don't even know when they are wrong. Really think they are right."

"There are many people who are doing holy things without being truly holy."

"Christians should not only 'talk the talk,' but should also 'walk the walk.'"

"Nothing is impossible, but some things are impractical."

*"It is unfortunate that so much unhappiness is contributed to poor communication."

*"A big communication gap can result from how much is said wrong and how much is heard wrong."

*"Being a good listener is admirable—but how do we know the listener has "heard" us if there isn't any verbal feedback?"

"We blame most of our hang-ups on our parents. Remember, they had parents too."

"There are two sides to every story. *And then there is the correct one."

"Remember, there are many who are doing the very best they know how, even though it may appear otherwise."

"No matter what the decade, the same good values should hold true."

"You can love an enemy without spending time with them or 'doing' for them. It is possible to love without commitment."

*"We should treat people civilly and not bitterly."

"Some people don't have a relationship with Christ. They have a religion."

"The only people who don't make mistakes are those who do nothing."

"People use the words 'forgive' and 'forget' as if they were the same word."

"It is in forgiving that we are pardoned and it is in remembering our past mistakes that allows us to grow for the better."

"If there are no struggles—there will be no spiritual victory."

"It is unfortunate that there are some people who don't start living until they are told they are dying."

*"It is quality above quantity that makes the difference in many aspects of life."

"Most young adults want adult privileges, but shirk adult responsibilities."

"An ounce of prevention is worth a pound of cure."

"Two wrongs don't make a right."

"Those who deserve love the least need love the most."

*"'Love' is for all—'Liking' is a choice."

"Any knowledge that isn't put to use is useless."

*"Outer appearances do not always reflect the truth of the soul."

"Even sinners love those who love them."

"Any man who does not yield his life to God is playing the fool."

"Our duty is not to see through each other, but we should see each other through."

"We should love people and use things. Some people love things and use people."

"The devil is at work when the creation takes on more importance than the Creator."

"If we are to master temptation, we must first let Christ master us."

*"There's a big difference between solitude and loneliness."

*"We learn by our mistakes is very often true. But mistakes due to carelessness or stupidity (with serious results) is NOT a way to learn."

"God's delays are not God's denials."

*"God is pleased when we give Him thanks, praise, or memorize scripture but, more importantly, He wants us to love His Son above all others and be doers of the word, NOT just hearers."

"In our times, insistence on obedience is often represented as an attempt to distort a child's personality."

*"There is 'good' logic and 'faulty' logic—and the only way to solve a problem is with valid (effective) solutions."

"Democracy is based upon the conviction that there are extraordinary possibilities in ordinary people."

*There is a definite difference between procrastination and patience.

"IT'S NOT THE INFORMATION—IT'S THE APPLICATION."

---

* Denotes personal quotes

After the Ascension

"In order that the human race may survive on this planet, it is necessary that there should be enough people in enough places in the world who do not have to fight each other, who are not the kinds of people who will fight each other and who are the kinds of people who will take effective measures whenever it is necessary to prevent other people's fighting."[68]

Above excerpt taken from the book entitled
The Mature Mind by:H.A.Overstreet.

---

[68]Excerpt taken from the book entitled *The Mature Mind* by H.A. Overstreet. Copyright 1959, W.W. Norton & Co., Inc., New York, NY.

M. GRACE FERRI

AMERICA THE BEAUTIFUL
(God Help Us)

The following italicized excerpts are taken from the magazine *Today*.

America, for the most part, is wrongly pursuing the gods of sex, money and humanism. When we become morally decadent, spiritually confused, politically corrupt and forsake God's commandments, God places nations under captivity.

"Blessed is the nation whose God is the Lord."
(Psalms 33:12)

In approximately 200 years the United States grew from infancy to greatness. And in approximately the last forty years the nation has begun a slide toward destruction. God honors and blesses those nations and people who honor and obey Him. It started in the 1960's when our country began to openly tolerate sin for the first time in her history. Then, in the '70's, we began to condone, legitimize and excuse those sins. We legislated immorality and passed legislation contrary to God's Word (The Bible). Government has been substituted for God and humanism for Christianity. Needless to say, too many people are living in natural carnal conditions.[69]

"The wicked shall be turned into hell, and all the
nations that forget God." (Psalms 9:18)

Our schools are no longer permitted to have **voluntary** *prayer. Evolution has been substituted for Creation and immorality for morality.*[70] *In too many cases, houses have been sub-*

stituted for homes, playboy fathers for godly dads, boisterous women for God-loving wives and mothers, along with unholy rebels for children not honoring parents. Nevertheless, teenagers need a base of support in the home, even though they may never articulate this need or understand it themselves. Humanism, for the most part, has destroyed all absolutes for the young. And what is very prevalent is religion without Christ and a possible future without God. Some 25 million or more little babies have been murdered through abortion—exceeding Hitler's holocaust of World War II.

> *"When the righteous thrive, the people rejoice; when the wicked rule, the people groan." (Proverbs 29:2)*

Motion pictures are too often "R" and "X" rated and television programming is perverting souls, brainwashing minds and destroying the spiritual life of our homes. So-called children's programs promote humanistic unholy ideas and subtly discredit morality and Christian values. Disrespect for authority is becoming rampant.

> *"Conduct yourselves in a way worthy of the gospel of Christ." (Philippians 1:27)*

Daytime dramas (the infamous soap operas) have become cesspools of filth, degradation and perversion. And then there is the tasteless commercials which tout sexually suggestive products like feminine hygiene products, birth control aids, women's and men's underwear (exhibiting indecent exposure and gestures), along with "Viagra," whose users could get out of control with probably half the elderly population going "crazy" over unnatural sex. This is not to say that this item could not be helpful for younger men with a problem.

The gambling casinos also advertise where, surely, too many are losing their homes, their savings, their household money, etc., and businesses are put in jeopardy. It is a pathetic situation for those who get out of control and not only lose their money, but lose their soul. Obviously, television advertising is not the only problem in regard to unhealthy and sinful ways.

Another enormous problem is pollution of our environment. Our waters are becoming polluted due to man's inconsiderate behaviors and the ozone layer is becoming more and more threatened. Scientists can do just so much to alleviate harmful conditions. An old time quote that should be heeded at all times is, "An ounce of prevention is worth a pound of cure."

> *"Those that honor me I will honor, but those that despise me will be disdained." (1 Samuel 2:30)*

Sex has become filthy and violent. Marketing companies are grossing thousands and thousands of dollars just on whips, chains and other bondage devices for the perverted. Unholy books and magazines are "over the top" in sales. There are far too many Americans enslaved to alcohol. Most of us are aware of the consequences of this sin. In addition, junkies and dope heads are too often bodies of America's young people.

And what about the internet? Our computers have become monsters for the "weak." All too often harmful contacts are made, whereby murders, rape, disgusting exchanges of conversations, etc. are coming into play. Our children need to be monitored and handled with a "tough love" for they are America's future citizens. We should be their holy parents and not concentrate only on being their best friend. Unfortunately, there are times when "good parenting" has unfavorable results.

PRAYER IS OUR GREATEST TOOL.

It has been said: "As a rule, the family that prays together, stays together."

An additional theory: "The family that eats together, stays together."

It is so unfortunate that the people of our country have become so luxury-loving and soft that they do not exert themselves to protect their cities or their standards. Wherein lies a nation that has abandoned the faith of its fathers. Here lies a people who also abandoned their priceless heritage of patriotism, religious faith and truth for socialism, sex and drugs. **However, thanks to God, not all Americans fit the above description,** *but, sadly enough, too many do! America[71] is the greatest civilization ever developed on this earth. Let us keep it this way.*

---

[69] Excerpts taken from the magazine *Today*, July/August 1993, Jack Vanimpe Ministries.

[70] If Darwin's theory is correct, why are apes still inhabiting the earth? Why didn't they evolve into humans??? (MGF)

[71] I can say in earnest that I love my country. I always did, from when I was a child. I sometimes become slightly tearful when I hear certain patriotic songs. I have tried to be a loyal American. Also, I salute the flag and pledge my allegiance to my USA. I am proud to be an American. (MGF)

M. Grace Ferri

SEPARATION BETWEEN CHURCH AND STATE

(A Definite Myth)

The following is from *The Myth of Separation Between Church and State* by Dee Wampler.

Amendment I

"Congress shall make no law respecting an establishment of religion, or prohibiting the free exercise thereof; or abridging the freedom of speech, or of the press; of the right of the people peaceably to assemble, and to petition the government for a redress of grievances."

The author of the phrase "separation of church and state" was never recognized as an authority on the First Amendment. This recent heavy reliance on Jefferson is a new and recent phenomenon. Jefferson was rarely cited by previous courts for reasons given by Jefferson himself.[72]

He was not part of the Constitutional Convention, and due to slow communications, any transmission of letters from him to the American convention would have required weeks. Jefferson rightly disqualified himself and although he wanted the Bill of Rights, he gave vague directions concerning it.

Jefferson's letter of January 1, 1802 was not a public policy paper, but a private letter. If private letters are to form the basis of national policy, then it would be important to pub-

lish all of the letter and thus provide its context rather than taking only eight words from it.

The First Amendment was never intended to separate Christian principles from government. The words "separation," "Church" or "State" are not found in the First Amendment and those phrases appear in no founding documents. The congressional records of June through September 1789 make it clear that they wanted God's principles, but not allow **one** denomination to run the nation. In 1799 the United States Supreme Court declared:

> "By our form of government, the Christian religion is the established religion and all sects and denominations of Christians are placed on the same equal footing."

From the beginning, European believers took a religious interest in America. In his very first entry in the diary that recorded Christopher Columbus' journey to America in 1492, he expressed hope he would make contact with native peoples in order to find out the manner in which may be undertaken their conversion to our holy faith. On his second journey in 1493, Columbus brought Catholic friars with the hope they could convert the Indians he had seen on his first voyage. **Columbus insisted profits from his voyage be used to restore Christian control over Jerusalem. Before his fleet set sail August 2, 1492, every man and boy confessed his sins and received absolution and communion.**

> "Neither reason nor mathematics—nor world maps were profitable to me, rather the prophecy

of Isaiah was completely fulfilled." (Christopher Columbus)

The Mayflower Compact written November 11, 1620, was America's great governmental document. It was signed by the Pilgrims before they disembarked their ship, the Mayflower. Beginning with the words "In the name of God, Amen" was the very first contract and government document ever entered "into" in our nation. This covenant was so revolutionary that it influenced every other constitutional instrument written since its time in America.

The Declaration of Independence was adopted July 4, 1776 and first read to the public at Independence Hall in Philadelphia four days later. By 1776, ninety-eight percent of all Americans professed to be Protestant Christians. **If this is not a Christian nation, how was it originally founded?**

Over a century ago, President Abraham Lincoln worried about our drifting away from God.

> *"That this nation, under God, shall have a new birth of freedom—and that the government of the people, by the people, and for the people shall not perish from this earth."*

*The Declaration of Independence might not be approved today as it is **politically incorrect**. It contains direct references to God and there is no indication that any delegate objected to such references.*

Today many Americans would protest the use of the word "Creator." It would be bemoaned by liberals as the endorsement of religion by government.

After the Ascension

On July 4, 1776, however, there was no debate over the phrase "endowed by their Creator" and that America was founded as a Christian nation with a constitutional government rather than a theocracy, but a Christian nation nonetheless.

The "Declaration of Independence" refers to the "Creator" rather than to Jesus and may be an acknowledgment that not all Americans of the day believed in the latter. In our nation's history, men and women have taken a stand for what is "right." They came to the New World seeking religious freedom and found that their faith in God played a role in many life changing decisions.

Over the past century, much of our religious heritage has been taken out of our history books and the influence which "faith in God" has in our lives and the lives of our forefathers is absent from public school classrooms today. We are in danger of losing our true heritage because the whole story is no longer being told. Our forefathers made a covenant with God and dedicated this land to the Lord.

> *"We need a great re-learning. We need to restore this nation's sense of greatness, to learn once again about the great deeds and the great men and women of our past so that we might move forward in the long journey towards moral reform and cultural renaissance in America." (Thomas Wolfe, Novelist)*

Of course, our founding fathers certainly were not angels and often did live by their own advice. If men were angels there would be no need for government. But their flaws, whether great or small, would hardly disqualify them to be used as guides to us today. Historical revisionists have erased their repeated references to and reliance on God. **There has never been a separation of church and state in our nation. Hopefully, there never will be.** It is not in our law now and was never intended to be a part of our law from the very beginning of our nation. There is an accommodation between the two, a close one that is permanent and longstanding.[73]

> "Whereas it is the duty of all nations to acknowledge the providence of the almighty God, to obey His will, to be grateful for His benefits, and humbly implore His protection and favor . . . " (George Washington)
>
> "All the good from the Savior of the world is communicated through this Book; but for the Book we could not know right from wrong. All the things desirable to man are contained in it." (Abraham Lincoln)
>
> " . . . the Bible . . . is the one supreme source of revelation of the meaning of life, the nature of God and spiritual nature and need of men. It is the only guide of life which really leads the spirit in the way of peace and salvation." (Woodrow Wilson)
>
> "The first and almost the only book deserving of universal attention is the Bible." (John Quincy Adams)

---

[72] Excerpts taken from the book entitled, *The Myth of Separation Between Church and State* by Dee Wampler. Copyright 2003, Winepress Publishing, Enumclaw, WA.

[73] It is quite evident that our forefathers never intended to have a separation of church and state.

After the Ascension

THE LETTER OF CONTROVERSY

Taken from *The Myth of Separation Between Church and State* by Dee Wampler.

On November 7, 1801, the Baptists of Danbury, Connecticut, wrote Thomas Jefferson wondering if their religious exercise was a government-granted right rather than a God-granted right. This was his reply:

To Messrs. Nehemiah Dodge and Others, a Committee of the Danbury Baptist Association, In the State of Connecticut:

> "Gentlemen,
>
> The affectionate sentiments of esteem and approbation which you are so good as to express towards me, on behalf of the Danbury Baptist Association, gives me the highest satisfaction. My duties dictate a faithful and zealous pursuit of the interests of my constituents, and in the proportion as they are persuaded of my fidelity to those duties, the discharge of them becomes more and more pleasing.
>
> Believing with you that religion is a matter which lies solely between man and his God, that he owes account to none other for his faith or his worship, that the legislative powers of government reach actions only, and no opinions, I contemplate with sovereign reverence that act of the whole American people which declared that their legislature should 'make no law respecting an establishment of religion, or prohibiting the free exercise thereof,' thus building a wall of separation between church and state. Adhering to this expression of the supreme will of the nation in behalf of the rights of conscience, I shall see with sincere satisfaction the progress of those sentiments which tend to restore to man all his natural rights,

convinced he has no natural right in opposition to his social duties.

I reciprocate your kind prayers for the protection and blessing of the common Father and Creator of man, and tender you for yourselves and your religious association, assurances of my high respect and esteem."

Today, all that is ever heard about Jefferson's letter is the phrase "wall of separation between church and state" without either the context or the explanation given in the letter or its application by earlier courts.[74]

---

[74] Taken from the book entitled, *The Myth of Separation Between Church and State* by Dee Wampler. Copyright 2003, Winepress Publishing, Enumclaw, WA.

After the Ascension

ANYWAY

(Treat People Like Winners)

People (can be) unreasonable, illogical and self-centered. Love them anyway.

If you do good, (some) people will accuse you of selfish ulterior motives. Do good anyway.

If you are successful, you (could) win false friends and true enemies. Succeed anyway.

The good you do today will (possibly) be forgotten tomorrow. Do good anyway.

Honesty and frankness make you vulnerable (which doesn't mean being tactless). Be honest and frank anyway.

People (usually) favor underdogs but follow only top dogs. Fight for some underdogs anyway.

What you spend years building may be destroyed overnight. Build anyway.

People (oftentimes) really need help but may attack you if you help them. Help people anyway.

Give the world the best you have and you'll (probably) get kicked in the teeth. Give the world the best you've got anyway.[75]

(Author unknown)

---

[75] Words in parentheses are personal emphases by M.G.F.

M. Grace Ferri

PEACE OF MIND
(Way to Go)

Peace is one of the most important and precious gifts that God has made available to us (through Jesus Christ). It doesn't happen overnight. **It takes time to learn how to make practical, Spirit led changes in our lives.** Many Christians are born again and baptized in the Holy Spirit, but still are lacking in complete peace because they are not striving to be obedient to the Lord. We are to search for peace and harmony (undisturbed by fears, agitating passions and moral conflicts) and seek it eagerly. We should *not* merely DESIRE peaceful relationships with God, with our fellow men, and with ourselves, but PURSUE (go after)them.

As previously mentioned many times, firstly, we should have a personal relationship with Jesus. Then we should stop rushing, set priorities, and live with "margins." In other words, besides striving to meet our obligations, we should leave room for prayer and relationships. **Changing our mindset is important.** Rushing and hurrying creates stress and stress is the root of many diseases. Also, we should seriously try to know our limitations. There are those who feel they have to "please" almost everyone they know. There is no way that we can be involved with everything and still remain cool, calm and collected.

Not everything that seems "good" is actually God's will for us to do. Very often something that seems "good" is the enemy of what God knows is best.

Another peace taking step is to acquire freedom from

financial pressure in any area. If financial pressure is robbing you of peace, ask Jesus for a specific plan to get you out of debt. Professional help should be pursued in severe cases. **To have financial prosperity one must give, save and spend within his or her means. To have financial prosperity and enjoy it, one must live within the word.**

We must slow down and take time to evaluate involvements. God did not create us to live our lives hurrying and rushing around from one thing to the next—- we were *not* made to exist under constant pressure and stress. He created us to live in PEACE.

Oftentimes, we envy others who have particular God given gifts or talents that we would like to have. God distributes His gifts and talents so everyone will *not* be the same. We should thank God daily for whatever blessings He has bestowed upon us and *not* envy others. There are many facets to achieving PEACE OF MIND and when we realize our limitations and go forward in the word, we will be taking a big step toward achieving peace. However, the ultimate adventure for a peaceful existence is to continue loving and trusting in God and following His Son, even when adversity strikes and we find ourselves on uncertain paths.

THREE DAILY REMINDERS

- HAVE THE COURAGE TO SAY "NO" (WHEN WE NEED TO).
- HAVE THE COURAGE TO FACE THE TRUTH.
- HAVE THE COURAGE TO DO THE RIGHT THING BECAUSE IT IS RIGHT.[76]

"He must turn from evil and do good; he must seek peace and pursue it." (1 Peter 3:11)

"Therefore, since we have been justified through faith, we have peace through our Lord Jesus Christ." (Romans 5:1)

---

[76] An overscheduled life is a life out of control. Usually the thing that suffers the most in a busy person's life is their relationships.

After the Ascension

BECOME A CHILD OF GOD

(A Last Stand On Becoming A True Christian)

Salvation has been offered to all, but it is up to each person to ACCEPT it in "this" life and to AWAIT its full realization in the "next" life.

A. We should accept the Bible as the word of God. We should have one in our possession and try to read it daily.
(Refer to Essay "It All Begins With The Bible")

B. It is only through the "grace of God" that we are saved, hence we must trust in God and pray for His grace (an unmerited gift) for He goes where He is wanted.[77] Only Born Again Christians will see the Kingdom of God. You can become Born Again no matter what Christian church you attend as it is a personal holy achievement.
(Refer to Essay "Grace")

C. Most importantly, in order to become "Born Again," we must accept and believe in Jesus Christ as our Lord and Savior, the only begotten Son of God, who died on the cross for our sins, was risen from the dead and ascended into Heaven to sit at the right hand of the Father.
(Refer to Essay "Transform Your Heart")

D. Then Jesus will turn our life completely around by keeping His commands through the Holy Spirit's power and get-

ting rid of all the "garbage" in us. We do this by sincerely confessing to Jesus and repenting. Oftentimes, repentance means facing the consequences of our sinful "ways" by making retribution to the laws of the land. However, we must be **truly** remorseful for our sins and **strive** never to sin again. Thus, we ask Jesus for His forgiveness as we forgive others.
(Refer to Essay "An Explanation of Repentance")

E. As we continue to grow in our personal relationship with Jesus, **making Him the center of our life,** He becomes our best friend with whom we share all our feelings, hopes and desires. We pray to Him for holy guidance, blessings and spiritual wisdom. He is our **only** "intercessor" to God.
(Refer to Essay "What It Means To Have a Personal Relationship With Christ")

F. Should we sin again because of our human weaknesses, we have the privilege to confess and repent over and over again and be forgiven by God as long as we are truly remorseful and strive to omit the sin. Jesus' suffering on the cross made this possible. He died with all the sins of the world weighted on His shoulders. God so loved the world that He allowed this to happen to save our souls. We should never take for granted what God has done for us.
(Refer to Essay "The Cross")

G. "Good Works" will count for salvation only **AFTER** we

have formed a personal relationship with Jesus. Good works and moral behavior are always important, but our love for Jesus is always **FIRST**. And because of our unconditional love for Him, we must always strive to follow His Father's Will, which means, of course, **making God's Son number one in our lives.**
(Refer to Essay "What Is Love?")

H. Prayer is a powerful tool, and we should take time to pray every day. It is possible to change people, including ourselves, through prayer. God answers all prayers one way or another, but we certainly have a better chance of God's favorable answer if we ask for His mercy, whereby admitting we are sinners, also repenting and asking for His forgiveness (as we forgive others). Even continuous sinners have "good things" happen to them on earth, but in the end their absence of following the "will of God" will cause them to encounter severe consequences by God.
(Refer to Essay "Regarding God's Will")

I. We should also pray to the Lord Jesus to give us a greater understanding of how "good" His good news really is and to give us the boldness to share this with others in a holy, mature and compassionate manner. **We should *not* only be "hearers" of the Word—we should be "doers" of the Word.**

God loves to be praised—but, more so, He expects us to share our Christian knowledge with others.

(Refer to Essay "Union With God Through Prayer")

J.   It is important to seek out a Bible teaching Christian Church and attend regularly. Also, to pay tithes, as it is in giving that we receive. God does *not* want us to make **foolish** sacrifices, financially or otherwise, in order to get returned blessings. These types of sacrifices could be categorized as misguided compassion. Family needs always come first.

(Refer to Essay "Transform Your Heart")

WE SHOULD STRIVE TO CORRECT THE ERROR OF OUR
WAYS BOTH SPIRITUALLY AND HUMANISTICALLY.
WE SHOULD REALIZE THAT REAL
COMMON SENSE MEANS TO KNOW THAT
GOD IS THE SOURCE OF WISDOM—
AND THE FINAL TEST OF LOVE IS
OBEDIENCE TO THE LORD.[78]

"Give, and it will be given to you . . . For with the measure you use, it will be measured to you." (Luke 6:38)

"Who then is greatest in the Kingdom of Heaven?" "Whoever humbles himself as this little child is the greatest in the Kingdom of Heaven." (Matthew 18:1–4)

"I am sure that God who began the good work within you will keep right on helping you GROW IN HIS GRACE until his task within you is finally

After the Ascension

*finished on that day when Jesus Christ returns."
(Philippians 1:6)*

---

[77] Holiness is *not* a matter of following rules, but of following Christ.

[78] Throughout the book I repeatedly state that God only goes where He is wanted. Paul was an exception through Divine Intervention and only God knows how many others.

M. Grace Ferri

INTRODUCTION TO THE BOOK OF REVELATIONS

The Book of Revelations was written by the Apostle John during his exile on the Island of Patmos. John's purpose in writing this book was to give hope and encouragement to those Christians who were suffering severe persecution for their faith in Jesus Christ.[79]

The framework of the Revelation is always a vision of hidden spiritual events; the language in which the vision is described is richly symbolic and so elusive that the message can be interpreted in more ways than one. This is the Revelation given by God through Jesus Christ so that He could tell His servants about the things which are soon to take place. Jesus Christ made it known to His servant, John, and John wrote down everything he saw. Happy are those who listen to Him, if they treasure all that it says, because the time is close.

The Revelation text contains difficulties; there are repetitions and interruptions. It must be understood first and foremost as a tract for the times written to increase the hope and determination of the church on earth in a period of disturbance and bitter persecution.

Godlessness In The Last Days

> *"But mark this: There will be terrible times in the last days. People will be lovers of themselves, lovers of money, boastful, proud, abusive, disobedient to their parents, ungrateful, unholy, without love, unforgiving, slanderous, without self-control, brutal, not lovers of the good,*

treacherous, rash, conceited, lovers of pleasure rather than lovers of God—having a form of godliness but denying its power. Having nothing to do with them." (2 Timothy 3:1–5)

---

[79] One of four interpretations of Revelations.

M. Grace Ferri

PRE-RAPTURE CONDITIONS

Before the second coming of Christ, there will be signs of a global economic collapse. Today, many jobs are being lost due to a new technical age of uncertain destiny.

Nuclear weapons capable of destroying all life on earth continue to be produced. China, with more than one-fourth of the world's population, continues to prepare for war.

Global weather patterns continue to change. Storms of unusual force strike in new places.

Lawlessness is rampant; murders continue to increase and no city is safe. Gang rapes occur while some average citizens look on and cheer. Jails are filled to overcapacity with criminals of all kinds.

Drugs are on the rise and increasingly connected with serious crimes. The use of drugs are way out of control. People are literally destroying their brains.

Family units are becoming more and more nonexistent.

Famines continue to expand over large sections of the world population. Volcanoes, long dormant, explode. Earthquakes continue to increase in frequency and severity, and then there are the tsunami disasters.

The above incidents are surely happening today. To the "**un**believer," this does *not* sound like the prelude to the coming of Christ to claim His Christian Church, the elect. But to the "Believer," this pattern clearly shows that the Lord's coming for His church is very near, according to prophecy.

After the Ascension

THE BELIEVER CAN SAY, "DO NOT STAND AT MY GRAVE AND CRY. I AM NOT THERE. I DID NOT DIE."

"No one knows about that day or hour, not even the angels in Heaven, nor the Son, but only the Father. As it was in the days of Noah, so it will be at the coming of the Son of Man." (Matthew 24:36)

"See, the day of the Lord is coming—A cruel day, with wrath and fierce anger—to make the land desolate and destroy the sinners within it." (Isaiah 13:9)

M. Grace Ferri

THE GROOMING OF THE ANTI-CHRIST

It is apparent that sometime before the rapture, which could very well occur at any time, the anti-Christ will be getting prepared by Satan to deceive the world by promising peace and trying to unite the world. Outwardly, there will be nothing wrong with uniting the world. The anti-Christ will gain the love and respect of many for his good efforts, but then the Rapture will come and naturally he will be left behind with the other multitude of **un**believers that preceded and followed him.[80]

After Jesus comes to claim His "elect," many of the **un**believers will reform and come to believe the truth. Hence, the anti-Christ will have to deal with the new Christians on earth. The anti-Christ will then reveal himself and his true goals and be opposed by the new Christians.

Unfortunately, these new Christians, who were given a chance by placing their faith in Jesus Christ, will *not* be able to escape the trials and tribulations that will come during this seven year period. There will eventually be ongoing wars between Christians and non-Christians. Earthquakes, mass murdering and nuclear warfare will exist. The rich will get richer, leaving the poor to struggle. There will be greed, and sin will be rampant among the **un**believers. One could believe that the Tribulation period and Armageddon will occur in the same seven year time slot.

After the Ascension

"He who has an ear, let him hear what the Spirit says to the churches. To him who overcomes, I will give the right to eat from the Tree of Life, which is in the Paradise of God." (Revelations 2:14)

---

[80]*There is someone in our midst today who is claiming to be of the "second coming" and also claiming to have approval of all religious heads to carry on with his plan for world peace. ("Beware, good people, for he has overtones of the 'Anti-Christ.' True Christians will know his real worth.")
*This information was taken from a full page article in The Providence Journal dated Saturday, July 6, 2002.

M. Grace Ferri

THE RAPTURE

(The Second Coming of Christ)

If you want to bypass the Rule of the anti-Christ and the most chaotic seven years the planet would ever see, start to prepare yourself immediately for True Christianity.[81] For Christ will come soon like a thief in the night. He will come down from Heaven as He ascended and His feet will *not* touch the ground. And with a wink of an eye, Christ will come to claim His Christian Church which consists of all Born Again Christians dead and alive. His angels will first sweep up the dead "In Christ" and they will rise in body form to meet Jesus in the sky. Secondly, the alive "In Christ" will be swept up in the same manner. All will leave their belongings behind. It will happen so fast that nonbelievers will *not* even get a glimpse of Him.

And who are the nonbelievers? They are the ones who question the Bible as being the True Word. The ones who leave Jesus out of their life. Some are in complete adoration of the canonized saints, forgetting that Christ died on the cross for us and for the sins of the world and that He "alone" is our Lord and Savior. Only the believers will see Christ and know what is happening. All babies and young children will be raised automatically because of their innocence. Unborn babies will be taken from the pregnant unsaved mothers. All the risen dead "In Christ" will be united with their souls. Those who are left behind will suffer the horrors of the Tribulation period.[82]

> *"For the Son of Man is going to come in his Father's glory with his angels, and then he will*

After the Ascension

reward each person according to what he has done." (Matthew 16:27)

" . . . That is how it will be at the coming of the Son of Man. Then two men will be in the field; one will be taken and the other left. Two women will be grinding with a hand mill; one will be taken and the other left. Therefore, keep watch, because you do not know on what day your Lord will come." (Matthew 24:39–41)

---

[81] Author made reference to the book entitled *Left Behind* by Tim LaHaye and Jerry B. Jenkins. Copyright 1995, Tyndale House Publishers, Carol Stream, IL.

[82] When we die, our soul/spirit immediately leaves our bodies and goes before Jesus for the first judgment. The second and final judgment is when Jesus comes again to claim His elect.

M. Grace Ferri

THE TRIBULATION PERIOD
(After the Rapture)

Right after the Rapture, where the dead and the alive "In Christ" will rise, there will be complete chaos on earth. Since this resurrection will happen in a wink of an eye, the **un**believers will see "nothing" other than many loved ones mysteriously missing.

Many of those left behind will most likely spread the word that aliens have invaded Earth. Others will blame nuclear warfare. Many theories will be exploited, but only some will know the truth from previous discussions and pleas by Christian loved ones. However, there will be some nuns, pastors and other clergy, etc., who surprisingly will be left behind. They will know "why" in their hearts for they will sadly realize that ***there are Good Christians and Better Christians***. They will know that the Lord left them behind because they were *not* fully in love with Christ. They knew about Him, but did *not* know Him personally. This group will then preach the true way—the right way—and lead many others to salvation after their own conversion. They will instruct those left behind, possibly giving them a second chance for God's Kingdom (which is to become Born Again).

In the meantime, it is unfortunate that these New Christians will have to face such tragedy and chaos. It will start with the True Christians being missing. Anyone who leaves a key position unoccupied will be the cause of car crashes, plane crashes, etc. Fires will result from nuclear plants where important positions will be left vacant. And through the seven years, earthquakes, fires, endless volcanic eruptions, nuclear wars and other disasters will take their toll. Also, many will be beheaded, for they were of God and did *not* possess the Mark of the Beast (666). Those who possessed the Mark of the Beast and worshiped the anti-Christ will be omitted from the sword slayings. But the Beast will be captured, and with his false prophet they will be thrown alive into the fiery lake of burning sulfur and be tormented day and night forever and ever. The remaining anti-Christ followers will be killed with the sword that comes out of the mouth of the rider on the horse and all the birds will gorge themselves on their flesh. After this holocaust, a New Heaven and Earth will come into being and Satan will be bound for 1,000 years.

> *"I will punish the world for its evil, the wicked for their sins. I will put an end to the arrogance of the haughty and will humble the pride of the ruthless." (Isaiah 13:11)*

M. Grace Ferri

ARMAGEDDON:

(AN INTERLUDE IN THE TRIBULATION PERIOD)

(Scene of the Battle Foretold in Revelations 16:14–16)

Some time after the initial horror of events occurring right after the Rapture (within the first half of the Tribulation period), the world will come to some sort of peaceful existence. Many **un**believers who were left behind will become believers, whereby having a second chance to live on with Christ. The non-believers, along with the anti-Christ, will suffer violently under the wrath of God.

But in the meantime, the world will worship the beast, the anti-Christ. First, the people will give absolute authority to the anti-Christ because of fear of war, and when Russia comes against the land of Israel, the Lord will declare His fury, anger and blazing wrath upon the wicked. This war will begin in the middle of the seven year Tribulation period. The nuclear war will escalate in stages until it becomes an all-out worldwide nuclear holocaust. It will be a war of God against the wicked.

God will remove any who willfully refuse to obey his righteous laws. After Armageddon, no part of this wicked world will remain. Only persons who serve God will continue to live. Satan and his demons will be gone.

God has *not* destined us for wrath, but for obtaining salvation through our Lord, Jesus Christ. After Armageddon (the second half of the Tribulation), there will be New Earth and a

After the Ascension

New Heaven, hence the millennium (1,000 years), which will be paradise on earth.

> *"Then I saw a new heaven and a new earth, for the first heaven and the first earth had passed away, and there was no longer any sea."*[83] *(Revelations 21:1)*

---

[83] The "sea" (biblically) could mean lost or bewildered.

M. Grace Ferri

THE MILLENNIUM

(Satan Is Bound For 1,000 Years)

After the seven year Tribulation Era, a New Heaven and a New Earth will come into existence. Jesus will descend from the Heavens with His angels and saints and with trumpets blowing; the saints being the Believers (the Elect) who were raised at the Rapture and the ones who turned to Christ at the Tribulation. This New Earth will have no natural disasters and will be free from all sin. The dwelling of the Lord will be with men and He will live with them. There will be chores for everyone. And the once wild beasts will be tame and act lovingly. Everyone will be completely healthy and no one will go without the necessities of life. No one will be overworked or overburdened, and all will live in peace and harmony.

There will be no marriages in Paradise, hence the population will *not* increase. Since God wants everyone completely happy, He most likely will blot out the memory of any loved ones who were left behind at the rapture. For how could we possibly be happy if we noticed certain cherished ones were missing from this Paradise?

> *"He will wipe every tear from their eyes. There will be no more death or mourning or crying or pain for the old order of things has passed away."*
> *(Revelations 21:4)*

In the "end" the New Earth will be as God wanted it in the "beginning" with Adam and Eve before they made their sinful choice against His will. And with the New Earth, His commandment will finally be fulfilled: *"Love one another as I love you."*

When the 1,000 years are over, Satan will be released from his prison and will go out to deceive the nations in the four corners of Earth to gather them for battle. They will march across the breadth of the earth and surround the "camp of God's people," the city He loves. But fire will come down from Heaven and devour them.[84]

> *"And the devil, who deceived them, was thrown into the lake of burning sulfur, where the beast and the false prophet (anti-Christ) had been thrown. They will be tormented day and night forever and ever." (Revelations 20:10)*

---

[84] The devil and his angels, the false prophet and the beast (anti-Christ) will be the ones who will suffer *forever*.

M. GRACE FERRI

JUSTICE FOR ALL

The following italicized text is an excerpt taken from the booklet, *The Three Greatest Sins* by Richard W. De Haan.

The Great White Throne

*The purpose of the Great White Throne is to determine the degree of punishment the **unsaved** will undergo throughout eternity. The "Book of Deeds" will be opened and the dead will be judged on the basis of what is recorded in these volumes. Those who, in their lifetime, were given greater light and more favorable opportunities or those who lived more wickedly than others will receive a punishment that is proportionately more severe.*

The unsaved who stand before the Great White Throne will also be confronted with the book of life. John says:

> *"... and another book was opened, which is the book of life." (Revelations 20:12)*

*In this volume are inscribed the names of all who are saved, and it evidently serves as a double check. Not only does the record of works condemn the **un**believers, but the very **absence** of their names from the "book of life" confirms the fact that the unbelievers never accepted the salvation God so mercifully offered. The names of all who received the Lord Jesus Christ will be in this book, but the names of the Christ rejecters will be missing. It is indeed a solemn thought that one's eternal destiny is determined by whether or not he accepts Jesus Christ.*[85]

---

[85]Excerpt taken from the booklet, *The Three Greatest Sins* by Richard W. De Haan, teacher of the Radio Bible Class Worldwide Ministries. Copyright 1971 by RBC Ministries, Grand Rapids, MI.

After the Ascension

PERSONAL SUMMARY

The previous pages on the Book of Revelations are my digested account of this book by John. The Holy Spirit has guided me as to the possible order of things. I was advised that there are actually "four" different interpretations of this "Book." I know many will feel I am not qualified to do this as I am not a Bible scholar, preacher, teacher, evangelist or theologian. I am only a high school graduate.

However, I have been privileged to see a vision upon awakening one morning in October 1978. The vision was a likeness of the picture in this book of the Ascension of Jesus. In the vision, Jesus' arms were outstretched upward and He was ascending. I eventually found a picture of this vision after searching for it for many years. The picture I found had "people" witnessing His Ascension. However, in my vision, the people were excluded. And in May 2003, just before awakening, Jesus appeared to me in a dream. His arms were outstretched beckoning me to join Him. I thought I had died and was thrilled to see Him, but then I awakened and I was happy to still be alive.

I have been truly slain in the spirit[86] by a Monsignor at a Catholic Charismatic rally. I had witnessed this "slaying" on television many times. Until I personally experienced this "spiritual slaying," I thought this action was a complete farce. Also, I was baptized in the Holy Spirit with evidence of speaking in tongues (February 7, 1983). I have loved God since I was a little girl. I knew **about** Jesus, but did not know Him **personally**. Much later, through listening to Christian preachers on television, radio and by attending Charismatic rallies, I grew in the Spirit and made Jesus the love of my life.

I am still growing, and by His grace, if I win but a handful of souls for Christ, I will be grateful. **I fully realize I am but a small link in a big chain of spirituality.** As children of God, the Lord wants us to pass on any spiritual knowledge that the Holy Spirit has given us.

GOD CONTINUES TO WORK THROUGH HUMAN BEINGS, ONE GENERATION AFTER ANOTHER.

"All this I do for the sake of the Gospel, so that I too may have a share in it." (1 Corinthians 9:23)

---

[86]"Slain in the Spirit" is a state of being spiritually slain when hands are placed on the forehead by a Christian Administrator. The Spirit-filled person spontaneously falls backwards and for a short period remains in a sleep-like state, at which time extreme peace and tranquility are experienced.

GLOSSARY

(Works of An Author With Its Immediate Context)

A

Abortion Many are concerned about the mistreatment of both wild and domestic animals, but they think nothing of the elimination of an unborn baby, which is murder in God's eyes. Do not sweep away an unborn baby like a disposable possession. Putting unwanted babies up for adoption can lovingly fill the needs of those who cannot have their own children.

Anger There is cruel anger and justified anger. Cruel anger is a sin—justified anger is *not*. Both should be restrained immediately to maintain order. We should be understanding and forgiving and try to communicate in a sensible fashion.

Armageddon The kings gathered together to the place called Armageddon to discuss the final and conclusive battle between the forces of good and evil.

B

Baptism According to the Bible, this is **not** an event for babies for they obviously are not mature enough to understand God's reasons for baptism. It is a Christian event marked by the use of water to purify and cleanse spiritually to symbolize faith in Christ. Jesus was thirty years old when he was baptized in the River Jordan by John the Baptist.

Bible What was written and recorded is the whole truth as it happened. However, ungodly ways that were practiced came under the wrath of God and He was *not* pleased. His Son came down to save the

	world, but, unfortunately, too many have *not* taken advantage of His gift of salvation.
Believer	One who believes in Jesus' atonement for his or her sins. Also, one who loves Jesus first in life and believes that He is the Son of God, that He died on the cross for our salvation, that He was risen alive into Heaven and will one day come again.
Blood	The precious blood of Jesus should have significant meaning to Christians for He freed us from our sins by His blood shed from the cross. God presented Jesus as a human sacrifice of atonement through faith in the blood of Christ. We can surely rebuke the devil by mentioning the blood of Christ in prayer.
Born Again	Also referred to as "Renewed in the Spirit," "Rebirth," "Saved" or "Born of the Holy Spirit." It involves the cleansing of the soul by confessing to Jesus, repenting and making Him the central figure of our lives. Only through Jesus can you enter the Kingdom of Heaven.

C

Compassion	Sympathetic consciousness of other's distress with a desire to alleviate it. Even sinners love those who love them. Hence, love is *not* restricted for the believers.
Compassion (Misguided)	When "good" is done for others at the expense of denying your family. God does *not* want us to make foolish sacrifices in order to get returned blessings.

D

Divine Intervention
: When God (often through His angels) compels or prevents an action—or alters a condition.

Divorce
: This is *not* the unpardonable sin as many believe it to be. However, it is a "sin" and like all sins, it can be forgiven if sincerely confessed to the Lord and repented. However, being truly remorseful of the situation is essential and, of course, treating each other civilly and *not* bitterly is the key to good relationships. God always hates the sin, but He always loves the sinner and we should do the same. (Refer to "Marriage" in this concordance).

E

Eye for Eye (Tooth for Tooth)
: This is from the Old Testament which is too often used for personal revenge. We should always settle our disputes in a God-like manner. In the New Testament Jesus said, *"You have heard that it was said 'Eye for eye, and tooth for tooth.' But I tell you, Do not resist an evil person. If someone strikes you on the right cheek, turn to him the other also. And if someone wants to sue you and take your tunic, let him have your cloak as well. If someone forces you to go one mile, go with him two miles. Give to the one who asks you, and do not turn away from the one who wants to borrow from you."* (Matthew 5:38–42)

The Lord does *not* appreciate revenge in any form. He advises to settle disputes out of court, otherwise you may be found unfairly guilty.

F

Fasting
: To eat sparingly or abstain from some foods, drinks or bad habits. Fasting occasionally is especially powerful when combined with prayer, edifying not

	only our bodies but our souls. The Lord is always pleased when we make sacrifices for Him.
Feelings	Feelings can either be right or wrong. One's thinking determines them. It is the **action** that counts. Negative or lustful feelings should be "nipped in the bud," so to speak. We can control our thoughts by prayer or by changing circumstances or by renewing our minds. Never let the devil win for there is too much at stake when we give in to him.
Forgiveness	The best way to heal a heart is to forgive (even the unforgivable). Holding a grudge (hating) over painful issues can cause many SERIOUS CONDITIONS affecting our health. Only when we forgive, will the Lord forgive us. The Lord's Prayer states: "Forgive us our trespasses as we forgive those who trespass against us."

G

God	"Supreme Being" whom we adore and love by "faith." His beauty envelopes the earth. In six days he created the Heavens and Earth and on the seventh day, the Sabbath, He rested. When God the Father, God the Son and God the Holy Spirit take an active part in our lives, inner peace and rest are available to us. Only through His Son Jesus can we enter the Kingdom of Heaven. *"For God so loved the world that He gave His one and only Son, that whoever believes in Him shall not* perish but have eternal life." (John 3:16)
Good	There are a multitude of people who are good. They follow the laws of the land and of the church. Unfortunately, many are eliminating the one ingredient for salvation and that is "our Beloved Jesus." If He is *not* the center of our daily lives, we could be flirting with damnation no matter how good we are.

Grace	A virtue coming from God. A particular moral excellence and God's unmerited favor toward man.

H

Homosexuals	Homosexuals are *not* all doomed sinners unless they become ongoing offenders. Therefore, with confession and repentance and **striving** to sin no more, they can also become God's favorite people. Celibacy is clearly in their favor. In many instances, Divine Intervention has been known to take place, whereby causing a complete Christian turnabout in their lives. Praying to the Lord for guidance and forgiveness is of great importance.

I

Integrity	Firm adherence to a code of moral values. A person who is honest and non-corrupt. Environment and parental upbringing play a big part in developing good and holy people. Churches and schools are trying to take on this responsibility, but are in desperate need of parental assistance.

J

Jesus (Son of God)	He was more than a great prophet, a teacher and a healer. He was the Son of God whose mission was to save the world by the forgiveness of sins. Jesus suffered immensely with the scourging, then nailed to the cross and died for our salvation. He was the first person to live, die and rise, never to die again. He ascended into heaven "alive" to be with His Father. When you consider how the calendar was based on His existence, He did leave an exceptional mark on the world. **The obedience to**

the Cross of Christ is the most important thing in our life.

K

Knowledge	Worth nothing unless it makes us a better person in our daily lives. Any knowledge that isn't put to use is useless. Maturity is *not* measured by intellect. It is measured by compassion, understanding and forgiveness.

L

Lazarus — Was the first person that Jesus raised from the dead. Lazarus was dead and buried in a cave for four days before Jesus performed this miracle. Previously, Jesus had found Lazarus as a poor beggar at the gate of a rich man's house. He was covered with sores and was looking for garbage to eat. Jesus then became Lazarus' best friend along with his sisters Mary and Martha.

Light — Has several definitions, but spiritually it means understanding the truths of the Bible. Jesus is known as the "Light of the World." Like a lighthouse that provides light for the darkened waters, Jesus provides light for darkened souls. Through His parables in the Bible, Jesus illuminates our hearts with love and by His example; He strengthens our faith in God His Father.

Lukewarm Christians — These are the ones the Lord finds the most fault with for He knows they know better, but they make up their own rules as to what is right and what is wrong spiritually. They favor the ways of the flesh and are oftentimes lacking regarding laws of the Spirit.

M

Magic Arts — The Lord seems to consider this art a very serious sin. Maybe because it is displaying seemingly supernatural qualities of powers and something that seems to cast a spell. The Lord does *not* believe that anyone should exercise supernatural powers over natural forces, for this is a falsehood and, of course, He advocates only the truth.

Marriage — It is the most difficult earthly relationship. Those who enter into marriage are committed to a lifetime relationship. We should always look for ways to redeem a marriage and to make it work. There are legitimate Christian reasons for divorce. (Refer to essay "Clean Up Your Act").

"For this cause a man shall leave his father and mother, and cleave to his wife." (Matthew 19:5)

N

Neighbor — We usually associate this word with those living close to us. However, Jesus used "neighbor" frequently. What He means is for us to treat our **fellowman** in a friendly, forgiving, loving and amicable way.

Nicodemus — The man Jesus talked to about being "Born Again" in order to see the Kingdom of God.

O

Overcome — To live in harmony with one another. Be willing to associate with people of low position. Do *not* be conceited. Do *not* take revenge. Leave room for God's wrath. Do *not* be overcome by evil, but overcome evil with good.

Orgies — Secret rites. Unrestrained indulgence in a group,

After the Ascension

especially with sexual activity. We should behave decently, *not* in orgies or drunkenness or sexual immorality or perversion. We should strive to **control** our thinking and actions in ways of gratifying the desires of our sinful nature.

P

Paradise — A place of bliss where complete happiness exists. Dwelling place of the Deity (God). A joyful abode of the **blessed dead**. Garden of Eden with no sin and everlasting life.

Pentecost — Outpouring of the Holy Spirit on the church to carry on the works of Christ after His ascension to Heaven. The Holy Spirit's gifts are definitely alive today. He and Satan are in a constant battle over souls. Tragically, thus far, Satan seems to be winning the battle.

Poor in Spirit — Being poor in spirit does *not* mean having "nothing." It means being free from earthly attachments and having a spirit that yearns for God's Spirit. This kind of "poor man" wants nothing which leads to sin and fervently seeks the friendship of Jesus and the desire to please Him more perfectly.

Predestined — Many believe that since their life is destined, fated or determined beforehand by God, there is little reason in striving to pursue an excellent life, for they feel "whatever will be, will be." The true spiritual meaning of "predestined" is the Doctrine that God, in consequence of His knowledge of all events, infallibly guides those who are DESTINED FOR SALVATION. God never plans ahead for bad things to happen to us. He gave us a free will, consequently, we are not programmed ahead like robots. Many times disasters come from our own wrong choices or somebody else's carelessness, serious mistakes, or wrong doings. Most of the time the devil is at work in these areas. However,

	there is a valid reason for everything God does. (Refer to Essay "Brokenness").
Pulpit	High reading desk used in preaching or conducting a worship service. The sermon from the pulpit should reflect powerful messages about the Christian truth of the Bible and what is necessary for salvation.
Purgatory	A very debatable plateau referred to in Catholic Bibles only. According to Catholic doctrine, a temporary place of torment and cleansing of souls to make them fit for Heaven. This second chance makes many Catholics lax in striving for the Kingdom of Heaven. Prayers are for the living. At our last breath, our state of spirituality is frozen. No prayers from loved ones left behind can help us thereafter. Only God can determine our fate. The "true" believer can say, *" . . . do not stand at my grave and cry, I am not there, I did not die."*

R

Repentance	To make a change. To walk away from ungodly ways. Repentance should take place immediately after sinning, *not* once a week.
Revelation (Book of)	Contains John's vision of the vindications in the world to come. This will be God's wrath against evil and He will exercise His power over all wickedness, whereby letting everyone know He is in full control and that His Son, Jesus, is King of Kings.
Righteous	Being right with God. It does **not** mean always being right humanistically. It means acting in accord with divine or moral law. Also, morally right or justifiable. Genuinely good.

S

Salvation
: Deliverance from the power of sin. To be saved. An unmerited gift by the grace of God. It is impossible to earn it. Doing good does *not* earn salvation. We should obey God because we love Him, *not* to earn His love, as He already loves us unconditionally. Before you receive the anointing of God, you have to be found faithful to Him—you have to hunger and thirst for righteousness.

Sanctification
: To purify. A state of growing in divine grace as a result of Christian commitment.

Satan
: The great enemy of man and of goodness. Known as the devil, Lucifer, Beelzebub, the Prince of Darkness and the chief of the fallen angels.

Sermons (Christian)
: Should be the center of awareness regarding our learning. When church sermons "offered" are lacking in spiritual direction, it is advisable to listen to Christian broadcasting in order to enhance our spiritual level. Of course, reading the Bible should be our first effort.

Sodom and Gomorrah
: Cities of ancient Palestine destroyed by God from rained down burning sulfur because of wickedness, and was rampant with homosexual practices.

Spare the Rod and Spoil the Child
: Where do we draw the line when it comes to making our children happy? Are we becoming slaves to their desires? Even the Bible says, *"Spare the rod and spoil the child."* God did *not* intend for us to beat our children. Serious and damaging punishment is *never* in order. Better to deprive them than to get out of control with physical punishment. However, up until the age of reasoning (seven), padded bottoms may warrant a **very slight** spanking. We should always be FAIR in decisions of punishment. Initial warnings (regarding wrongdoings) should always precede acts of punishment.

T

Talent — God distributes talents in many ways. Some people have more than others. God gets upset with those who do *not* focus on their special God-given aptitudes, but instead bury their gifts because of laziness and/or slothfulness.

U

Unforgiving Spirit — We should deal with problems as soon as possible, otherwise bitterness and anger will turn into hatred. God will *not* forgive you unless you forgive others.

Unleavened — A kind of bread containing no yeast that was used by Jesus at the Last Supper.

V

Virtues — A moral goodness. A particular moral excellence. Also relating to Kingdom of God or Divinity.

W

Warnings — All of us encounter warnings in our lifetime. The wise person heeds warnings—the foolish ones too often disregard them. There are repeated warnings in the Bible that could affect our salvation but are oftentimes rejected by many Christians.

Womb — First we are born through our mother's womb. We become "Born Again" through the Baptism of the Holy Spirit.

Y

Yoked — *"Be not yoked together with an unbeliever."* (2 Corinthians 6:14) This does *not* mean we must marry someone of the same race, color or denomination. It means that believers should *not* be matched with **un**believers. When both parties are Christians, God will show them the way.

Z

Zion — Citadel in Palestine which was the nucleus of Jerusalem. The Jewish people: Israel. The Jewish homeland that is symbolic of Judaism or of Jewish national aspiration. The ideal notion or society envisioned by Judaism.

M. Grace Ferri

JESUS

"I'M SO GLAD HE CAME INTO MY LIFE."

M. Grace Ferri

A PERSONAL ANALYSIS

It came to mind that our beloved Jesus could *not* have been a tall, good-looking man as usually depicted. For if it were so, He most likely would have been followed and worshipped by many solely for His sex appeal (as many performers are today) rather than for His holiness and spiritual teachings (parables). Jesus also wanted people to "believe" on the evidence of the miracles that He was truly the Son of God (John 14:11). Shortly **after** coming to the conclusion of His cosmetic appearance, I ironically came upon the following in my Bible:

> *"He had no beauty or majesty to attract us to him, Nothing in His appearance that we should desire him." (Isaiah 53:3)*

"Finally, all of you, live in harmony with one another; be sympathetic, love as brothers, be compassionate and humble. Do not repay evil with evil or insult with insult, but with blessing, because to this you were called so that you may inherit a blessing." (1-Peter 3:8–9)

ABOUT THE AUTHOR

(The Transition)

Born in Providence, Rhode Island, March 7, 1927. Married my teenage sweetheart, John Ferri, in October 1950. We have four sons, twelve grandchildren and two step-grandchildren.

*I was a "Catholic Christian" for **many** years until one morning, while convalescing in bed (due to a back problem), the 700 Club with Pat Robertson automatically came on television. Because of my back problem, I could not move to change the channel. At the time I was appalled because Catholics are not supposed to participate in anything that isn't Catholic. After watching this program the first time, I got "hooked" and watched it from my bed for the five weeks that I convalesced.*

Stemming from this television program, I began watching Charles Stanley, Jimmy Swaggart and other Christian broadcasting. Consequently, I learned more about Christianity than ever before (I'm still growing and will continue to grow until the day I die). However, if I had not heard Jimmy Swaggart preaching about the Spiritual Gifts, including "Speaking in Tongues," I would have thought I was going "mad" when I received this Spiritual Gift, as I was never made aware of these gifts. The "words" were read from the Catholic pulpits, but never explained. I was recently exposed to Joyce Meyer, a Christian preacher on television, who has greatly enhanced my spiritual awareness.

At one time I was leaning toward becoming a "Protestant Christian" until I asked myself the question, "If the Protestants believe that only the souls of the 'Born Again Christians' go to Heaven and the 'evil' go to hell, where do all the other souls of the departed go, the souls of those who were good but not good enough for Heaven and not evil enough for hell?" Hence, I could not "let go" of the "so-called" Catholic Purgatory—a level of Heaven that I perceive quite differently than the Catholic Church does (refer to essay entitled "Three Heavens").

I am now "A Born Again Christian" attending (along with my husband) Old St. Mary Church, the oldest standing Catholic Church in Rhode Island, **in hopes that the Catholic Church will one day realize the error of its ways** and become a complete follower of the Bible (probably not in my earthly lifetime).[87]

In conclusion, due to my manic-depressive condition, I took Lithium for over 20 years. Three and a half years ago, one of my sons (a Born Again Christian) encouraged me to experiment with eliminating the Lithium in order to find out if I still needed it. Consequently, through his prayers and God's Divine Intervention, I have been healed since November 2001.

M. Grace Ferri[88]

"Blessed are those who hunger and thirst for righteousness for they will be filled." (Matthew 5:6)

---

[87] For more about the author, refer to "Personal Summary" (after Revelations).

[88] I did not personally choose to be called "Grace." It was handed down to me. My paternal grandmother's name was Maria Grazia Calise, which is the name on my birth certificate. Translated into English it is "Marie Grace." However, she was forever called by her second English name, hence, I was called "Grace" from birth.

M. GRACE FERRI

THE GRACE OF THE LORD JESUS CHRIST,

THE LOVE OF GOD,

AND THE COMMUNION OF THE HOLY SPIRIT

BE WITH ALL OF YOU

INDEX

About the Author 231
After the Resurrection 130
Agony in the Garden 122
America the Beautiful 177
Angels 70
Anger 76
Anyway (Treat People Like Winners) 188
Apostle Paul 133
Apostle Paul (Meeting With Jesus) 135
Armageddon (An Interlude in the Tribulation Period) 207
Arts and Virtues 73
Ascension, The 132
Baptism 110
Beatitudes (Sermon on the Mount) 113
Become a Child of God 192
Biblical Quote From Peter 3:8–9 230
Birth of a Theory (Three Heavens) 161
Book of Revelations, Introduction to 197
Born Again Christian 43
Brain, The (Good Health Tips) 157
Brokenness 34
Clarification of "Born Again" or "Saved" 43
Clean Up Your Act 90
Cross of Christ, The 124
Devil Attacks Us, The 57
Does God Heal Today? 37

After the Ascension

Emperor's Feat	31
Evil	60
Explanation of Repentance	48
Friends	79
From Tradition to Truth (Former Priest)	154
Glorious Experience (Holy Spirit)	25
Glossary	215
God Sent Us a Savior	106
God Speaks in the Bible	18
God's Plan to Carry on His Son's Teachings	21
Good Judgment in God's Service	61
Grace	50
Grooming of the Anti-Christ	201
Hail Mary	67
How Could We? (Poem by M. Grace Ferri)	102
Human Race, The	176
Is Your Mouth Saved?	46
It All Begins With The Bible	15
Jesus Promises The Holy Spirit	23
Jesus Teaches Nicodemus	42
Justice For All	211
Knowledge and Order	81
Last Supper, The	120
Let Him In (Poem by M. Grace Ferri)	104
Letter of Controversy, The	186
Lord's Prayer	66
Love (1-Corinthians 13:1,4)	82
Mary Was Chosen	107

Millennium, The	209
Peace of Mind	189
Personal Analysis, A	229
Personal Relationship With Christ, A	52
Personal Summary	212
Picture of Ascension	20
Picture of the Cross	123
Picture of Jesus	227
Picture of the Last Supper	119
Prayer of Saint Francis of Assisi	68
Prayer to God	63
Pre-Rapture Conditions	199
Priesthood (Catholic)	152
Prisoners of Childhood	98
Quotes, Favorites	172
Rapture, The	203
Rebirth of a Theory (Uncharted Territory)	167
Regarding God's Will	54
Reincarnation	167
Repentance	48
Resurrection, The	128
Right and Wrong, Roman Catholicism (Essay)	139, 142
Right and Wrong (Poem)	138
Saved	43
Separation Between Church and State (A Complete Myth)	181
Sermon on the Mount (Beatitudes)	113
Sins	90
Speaking In Tongues	29

Summary of Three Heavens (A Hypothesis)	163
Taste and Style, Roman Catholicism	146
Ten Commandments, The	88
Transfiguration, The	116
Transform Your Heart	39
Tribulation Period, The	205
Turn Your Life Around (Poem By M. Grace Ferri)	103
Union With God Through Prayer	64
Variety and Unity of Spiritual Gifts	27
Wake Up Call, A	100
What Is Love?	83
Three Kinds of Love	84
Love and Marriage	86
Who Killed Jesus?	127
With God All Things Are Possible	160

Contact author M. Grace Ferri
(401) 821-8705
or order more copies of this book at

TATE PUBLISHING, LLC

127 East Trade Center Terrace
Mustang, Oklahoma 73064

(888) 361 - 9473

Tate Publishing, LLC

www.tatepublishing.com